HQ767.15 .A27

ABORTION

My Choice,
God's Grace

ABORTION

My Choice, God's Grace

Christian Women Tell Their Stories

Anne Eggebroten
Editor

New Paradigm Books
Pasadena, California

"Cracking Up—Or Coping" is adapted from "How I Faced Reality" which appeared in the June 1980 issue of *TheOtherSide,* 300 W. Apsley, Philadelphia, PA 19144 and is reprinted with permission.

For information address:
New Paradigm Books
P. O. Box 60008
Pasadena, California 91116 - U.S.A.

Cover design - Michael McClary/The Workshop

Printed in the U.S.A. on acid-free paper.

Library of Congress Cataloging-in-Publication Data

Abortion--my choice, God's grace : Christian women tell their stories
   / Anne Eggebroten, editor.
      p.   cm.
   Includes bibliographical references.
      ISBN 0-932727-79-0 : $19.95. -- ISBN 0-932727-69-7 (pbk.) : $12.95
      1. Abortion--United States--Moral and ethical aspects.
   2. Abortion--United States--Religious aspects. I. Eggebroten, Anne Marie.
   HQ767.15.A27   1994
   363.4'6--dc20
                                                          94-3062
                                                          CIP

For women
who have died
for the right to choose

Table of Contents §

Acknowledgments §

As I think back on whom to thank for help with this book, the words of a song I sang every week at Young Life meetings during my high school years come to mind: "On Christ the solid rock I stand—all other ground is sinking sand ... "

I am convinced God wanted this book to be and sustained it against overwhelming odds. Certainly there were enough factors working against its completion. *Abortion: My Choice/God's Grace* was conceived when I was three weeks pregnant and had a four-year-old and a two-year-old. Somehow the book got started in spite of diapers, cooking and cleaning. When the book was one year old (and my youngest daughter was three months old), I took a full-time teaching job that lasted two years.

The next year I stopped teaching to work on the book, but somehow I found myself on the sinking sand of leading a Brownie troop. Outings, cookie sales and weekly meetings in our home demanded and got much more of my time than the book. Then a financial pinch led to full-time teaching again for the last three years, leaving only summers to work on the book. But summers often went to planning workshops or speakers for conferences of the Evangelical and Ecumenical Women's Caucus. Selling a home and moving, deaths in the family, and even earthquakes have kept me from working on this book.

Therefore, my thanks go first to God for sustaining this book through all these obstacles.

I also want to thank my contributors and the network of biblical feminists that put me in touch with each of them. Finding

Christian women able to talk and write about their abortions was difficult, but it was made possible by the existence of groups such as the Evangelical and Ecumenical Women's Caucus, Daughters of Sarah, and Catholics for Free Choice. I particularly thank each of the contributors for your honesty and courage.

Finally I want to thank my publisher, Faith Annette Sand, for her patience with this project and her courage in bringing out a book on abortion at a time when extremists have resorted to stalking and murder. Her financial courage is notable, too. Several publishers turned down the book for its unique marketing problems: it is designed primarily for those Christian who oppose legal abortion, yet those same people would be unlikely to buy a pro-choice book, however moderately or mildly written. We are trusting that many pro-choice people will buy the book, read it, and pass it along.

All of this brings me back to the grace of God. After a very biblical seven years of work and diversions (like Jacob's work for Leah, and then for Rachel), this book has entered the world. Thanks be to God.

Santa Monica, California
February, 1994

Foreword §

Bunnie Riedel

Founding Director,
Religious Coalition for Abortion Rights, Southern California

There are two great myths involving abortion. One myth is that abortion is always an easy decision. The other is that Christian women, particularly those in fundamentalist churches, do not have abortions. Having spent the last few years embroiled in the abortion debate, I can state without reservation that these two great myths have no basis in fact.

Abortion is almost always a difficult decision, no matter how much bravado a woman displays. I am continually awed by the spiritual struggle women go through as they face the decision; their introspection is admirable, and their anguish is quite real. I have talked to many women about their journey toward abortion, and it frequently stands apart from most of their other life experiences as uniquely difficult. However, I have also found that once a woman makes the decision to terminate a pregnancy, she is quite sure that she is doing the best thing, given her current life circumstances. That same woman in a different time and space might make a different decision.

More than anything else, being able to choose and being affirmed in that choice gives a woman peace. Knowing that God is with her in the abortion decision and that the church upholds her moral authority to make the decision brings a woman into deeper communion with the One from whom all life springs. It becomes a part of that list of things that cannot separate us from the love of God.

There is no doubt that Christian women have abortions. When Christian churches (whether Catholic, Orthodox, fundamentalist, charismatic or mainline Protestant) choose to go about their business as if none of the women in *their* pews are having abortions, they are engaging in spiritual violence. The damage they inflict on their own members is immense.

Each of the Christian faith groups which oppose abortion has its own reasons for trying to convince parishioners that abortion is something done by women who are not a part of their own faith group. The Roman Catholic Church is currently quite vocal in its opposition to abortion, although Catholic women have a higher rate of abortion than any of the other faith groups. As long as there are no women priests, bishops, archbishops or popes, we can expect opposition to both contraception and abortion to continue. The growth of the Catholic population is another factor. Accepting contraception is probably inevitable over the next hundred years, but it may result in smaller congregations. Some of the fundamentalist and evangelical churches, on the other hand, approach the abortion issue as a way to get people excited. The complexity of each woman's choice is reduced to a simplistic contest between "Christians" and "abortionists." Predominantly male leadership in these churches is certainly a factor in the oversimplification of this approach. Most mainline Protestants handle the abortion issue by avoidance. They know in their hearts that women in their pews are having abortions, but they avoid talking about it during church services or meetings. The unspoken message is, "Maybe we can just stick to the lectionary, not have any controversy, go home to Sunday dinner, come back for Wednesday night potluck, and still be good chums." Many women in these churches need guidance, support and sharing on this issue, but for the most part they aren't getting it.

In the meantime, women of all denominations fill the pews. They keep the doors open; the kitchens clean; the Sunday schools operating; the mission dollars flowing; the choir full; the baptisms occurring; the weddings, funerals and Christmas plays happening. But many of them also bear a secret. They feel that they would be rejected by other church members if anyone knew of their abortion. These women give much but are cheated out of the full acceptance and healing they deserve. Instead, they listen in silence as abortion is called "murder," or, worse, not talked about at all.

Count up half of the women in any Catholic church on Sunday morning and one out of three in the Protestant churches, and you're counting the women who have had abortions. Then think about their mothers, their aunts, their sisters, their nieces, their cousins, and their neighbors—many of whom have had abortions. Almost half of the women in the U.S. will have an abortion at some time in their lives. That's not just because abortion is legal: in Brazil, where abortion is illegal and the population is about half that of the U.S., there are twice as many abortions per year as in the U.S. After all, women are fertile for 30 to 40 years of their lives and the likelihood of their having an unacceptable pregnancy during that period is quite high. How many of us can manage anything perfectly for 30 years? Yet many expect *every woman* to get through all those years without an unplanned pregnancy.

In this book Anne Eggebroten has brought together personal stories that will begin to lift the fuzzy nonsense of our myths about Christian women and abortion. Yes, we who believe in Jesus Christ, who take communion or share the Eucharist, are flesh and blood. We have made mistakes and have found ourselves pregnant at times when this news was most unwelcome. We have struggled with decisions and have anguished over their implications for our souls. Many of us have discovered that God's love for us carries us confidently forward and through the abortion experience. We have discovered that the ability to make a decision about our pregnancy as a co-creator, rather than a passive vessel, gives us strength in other areas of our lives.

The sharing that takes place in this book needs to be done for the sake of all women, whether Christian or not, who have been psychologically and spiritually abused by the institutional church. Some of the stories here will relate to your own experiences, others will not—but in all of them you will sense each woman's distinct humanity and spirituality. You may even feel the conviction that we in the church—all of us who serve Jesus Christ—are not free of sin. That would be good to admit publicly; it is time that we come out of our darkness and into the light.

Read this book and share it with a friend. Pray over it, reflect upon it and then do something to make sure that abortion remains safe, legal and accessible to all women regardless of age or economic status. Speak up in your church and in your community. Let people know that you are a pro-choice Christian. If being actively pro-choice is not where God is leading you, work for better family planning services and education in your community to lessen the incidence of abortion. But above all, as

Christians, let us stop judging others.

Abortion is never an easy decision. Faithful Christian women choose to have abortions. Yet through all of our struggles, nothing—absolutely nothing—can separate us from the love of God.

Introduction §

Anne Eggebroten

The bride lay on the ground in her blood-soaked wedding dress. Nearby lay the ex-boyfriend who had shot her and then committed suicide. The groom was hysterical and the bride's mother had fainted. Children huddled with their parents near the home where the wedding reception was beginning in a suburb of Los Angeles. Police arrived to find Iliana Valencia Perez dead and her ex-boyfriend dying.

Iliana had just finished her first year at the private college where I teach. She had a lot of dreams for her future and was working hard to achieve them. But she was not allowed the right to choose a husband or a life for herself. One man not only took away her choices but her life; the restraining order she had obtained against him because of his threats had not protected her.[1]

Iliana is only one of many women who have died for the right to choose their own lives. The news is full of stories like hers. Every day some man somewhere takes the life of a woman— usually someone he thinks he owns. Husbands and boyfriends

---

[1] Maura Dolan, "Instead of a Life Together, Man Must Bury His Bride," *Los Angeles Times* 1 June 1993, B1.

kill more than 34% of all women murdered in the U.S.[2] Other men don't kill but govern the life of a woman through violence; still others rape a woman, taking away her right to make her own sexual choices.

Sometimes a man merely meets a woman and thinks he can govern her choices. Two weeks after Iliana died—and 3,000 miles away—Lisa Bryant graduated with honors from Princeton University. A few days later she reported to Fort Bragg in North Carolina to fulfill a commitment to ROTC, which had paid for part of her college education. But on July 10 she met an officer in a bar on her army base and refused his advances. Though she left the bar and returned alone to her room on the base, within an hour he attempted to rape her—and killed her.

Most of us are not denied the right to choose in such a drastic manner. But if we think of our mothers and grandmothers, we recall serious ways in which the choices in their lives were limited. Only 80 years ago women in the United States did not have the right to choose their government through the ballot box. A century before that, women did not have the right to choose a college education. As recently as the 1930s most women did not have the opportunity to choose contraception.[3] Even today Catholic women do not have that option if they are faithful to the teachings of their church.

The suffragists are history now and we think, "How strange that anyone would not want women to vote!" When we read

---

[2] *Crime in the United States: Uniform Crime Reports* (Washington, DC: FBI, US Government Printing Office, 1988 and 1989).
[3] Rosalind Pollack Petchesky, *Abortion and Woman's Choice: The State, Sexuality, and Reproductive Freedom* (Boston: Northeastern Univ. Press, 1984) 89-95.

about the intense opposition that Margaret Sanger met, we wonder how anyone could deny women the right to use a contraceptive. The struggle for full equality for women has shifted to other grounds: the right to be free from sexual harassment, the right to equal pay for equal work, the right to live without fear of violence or rape. We are now working for things that earlier women never dreamed of: low-cost health care, child care that is accessible and good, family leave to have a baby or to care for a parent without losing our jobs.

Procreative Choice

We are also working for full procreative choice—the idea that women should be able to choose when to bear children and that every child should be a wanted child. To have choice in this area, women need not only contraceptives but access to safe, legal abortion if they find themselves with a pregnancy that they cannot complete. In 1993 Dr. David Gunn died for his help in giving women access to full procreative choice.[4]

Traditionally, American soldiers have fought for the right to choose their own form of government. Today men and women in the United States and around the world are dying to secure procreative choice. Men and women are risking their lives to flee China, where abortion and sterilization are forced after one child (or two in certain rural areas), in a government attempt to curb population growth.[5]

---

[4] Paul Gray, "Thou Shalt Not Kill," and Richard Lacayo, "One Doctor Down, How Many More?" *Time* 22 March 1993: 44-47.

[5] Nicholas D. Kristof, "China's Crackdown on Births: A Stunning, and Harsh, Success," *New York Times* 25 April 1993: 1.

In Poland and other former Soviet block nations, abortion used to be the primary birth control method because reliable contraceptives were so scarce; however, Poland recently adopted a new law making abortion a crime except in cases of rape, fetal deformity or danger to mother's health.[6] Whether abortion is forced or denied, women and men who are denied full procreative choice are risking their lives for the opportunity to determine their own lives.

The U.S. Supreme Court ruled in 1973 that women have the right to choose an abortion in the first three months of pregnancy; after that point, states have the right to regulation based on the woman's health or the viability of the fetus. As we know, however, the *Roe* v. *Wade* decision was not the end of the story.

In the 1970s organized opposition to abortion began and grew prominent in the news (as well as opposition to the Equal Rights Amendment to the Constitution passed by Congress in 1972). Most of those opposing legal access to abortion (as well as those opposing the ERA) claimed that their position was rooted in Scripture. Actually, the word *abortion* is never mentioned in the Bible and the church did not oppose abortion in the first trimester for many centuries.[7] Life was considered to begin with "quickening" (the time a woman begins to feel the child move within her, in the fifth or sixth month).

During the 19th century and through the first half of the 20th

---

[6] "Back to the '50s: Poland," *Conscience: A Newsjournal of Prochoice Catholic Opinion* 14.1-2 1993: 56-57.

[7] D. Gareth Jones, *Brave New People: Ethical Issues at the Commencement of Life* (Grand Rapids, MI: Eerdmans, 1985) 173. See also Jane Hurst, *The History of Abortion in the Catholic Church: The Untold Story* (Washington, DC: Catholics for A Free Choice, 1989).

century, fertility control (including abortion) "was a domestic, 'home-made' affair, not at all within the province of physicians."[8] As of 1860, one doctor estimated that women, sometimes assisted by midwives, ended one in five pregnancies. At about that time the newly founded (and all-male) American Medical Association began trying to define and outlaw the practice of abortion, and eventually most states enacted laws prohibiting abortion except to save a woman's life.[9]

Right-wing Christians, however, have been successful in promoting the idea that abortion is and has always been wrong as far as religion is concerned. This misconception still persists, but surveys show that *most Americans of faith are pro-choice.*[10] In fact, 46% of American women will have an abortion by age 45, according to a 1992 survey, and that figure must include many Christian women.[11] Christians in difficult circumstances have been having abortions for centuries--long before abortion became legalized in the United States, and in fact long before it ever became illegal.

Christian Women Choosing Abortion

Every year thousands of women in conservative, born-again congregations find themselves in difficult situations where they choose abortion as the least painful or most responsible decision.

---

[8] Kristin Luker, *Abortion and the Politics of Motherhood* (Berkeley: Univ. of Calif. Press, 1984) 51-52.

[9] Petchesky, 78-79.

[10] "Bring the Word Home: Most Americans of Faith Are Pro-Choice," *Religious Coalition for Abortion Rights Newsletter* 20.1 (1993): 3.

[11] Nancy Nord Bence, "Filling the Need for Religious Support of Women," *RCAR Newsletter* 20.1 (1993): 2. See also Richard Lacayo, "Abortion: The Future Is Already Here," *Time* 4 May 1992: 28.

Most hide their choice from the church, but when a woman has enough courage or desperation to open up to her pastor or Christian friends, she often finds that she is no longer welcome at meetings and worship. Forgiveness and salvation by grace do not apply to certain sins.

The women in Part 1 have opened their lives to you, sharing their stories so that you will understand three things: 1) Christian women—deeply committed to their faith in Jesus Christ as Lord and Savior—sometimes find themselves with an unplanned pregnancy and choose abortion. 2) Most never imagined they would face this choice; they are distressed and in need of prayer and spiritual counseling. 3) They make their decision thoughtfully and prayerfully, based on their health and needs and on the welfare of the baby that would be born.

These are hard truths to face. It is much easier to live in a world where we can believe that: 1) True Christians don't have abortions or get in situations where they would even consider one. 2) Churches need to focus on saving the unborn (not on the needs of women). 3) Abortion is a selfish decision.

So many Christians want to stay in a world where these myths are considered to be true. But some people who take their faith seriously are ready to move beyond the "milk" of infant faith (described by Paul in 1 Corinthians 3) to become more mature Christians, facing the reality around them. If you are ready to challenge and strengthen your faith in this way, the personal stories of this book await you.

The women in Part 1 each decided to end a pregnancy, though many people around them believed that such a choice was morally wrong. As a result, most of these women experienced guilt. They began to work through that guilt, and in the process they encountered grace. They found a God who values *their* lives, not just the life beginning within them. They found that the Creator of the Universe can handle the loss of that potential life much better than some people on earth. Straining at the gnat of that tiny life, some Christians will swallow any violence toward the woman, her doctor or her clinic.

The stories in these pages show women of faith earnestly making difficult choices—one as a result of rape, others as a result of seduction, failed birth control or teenage mistakes. Two of the stories are about women whose physical health was so impaired they felt they could not complete a pregnancy and produce a healthy child. Another story is about a woman whose mental health was so precarious that having a child at that point in her life would have been a disaster both for her and for the child.

What is striking about these stories, however, is the healing and grace they reveal. Many of these women experienced a point of very low self-esteem, some even wanting to die, expecting God to abandon them as the church had. But later these women came to understand that God desires their healing and that an abortion can be part of that healing. Also striking in these stories is the unchristian, unkind behavior of many of the people surrounding these women. In rare cases, a boyfriend or husband offered real support to the woman he had unintentionally made pregnant. In even rarer cases the parents, friends, pastors and church family supported the woman enough that she could seek help. In only one story in this book does the woman receive unconditional acceptance from both her partner and her pastor; not surprisingly, this woman's story is the most matter-of-fact and guilt-free.

Yet grace abounds in the pages of this book, along with the

guilt. The grace that these women offer toward the men in their lives, toward their parents and toward the children in these stories is abundant. It is not news that we all are sinners; the good news is God's tremendous love and forgiveness toward us as manifest in the life and death of Jesus of Nazareth.

In Part 2 women of faith discuss abortion from other perspectives. In the early decades of the 20th century Marillia Hinds and the Reverend Anna McD. Miller heard the stories of abortions undertaken by saintly grandmothers and aunts; as a young girl in the 1930s, Marillia assisted in her mother's choice to have an abortion. In pastoral counseling, Mary Helen Spencer has aided young women recovering from rape and seduction in church youth groups. Sally Carpenter assisted as an escort in an abortion clinic that was being attacked by anti-abortion activists, and later she participated in the March for Women's Lives in Washington, DC, in 1992. Faith Annette Sand recounts experiences that led her to place the words "Judge not, lest ye be judged" ahead of any absolute statements about when life begins. In the last chapter, I share the story of my unwanted pregnancy and how I considered abortion but finally chose to have the baby—grateful that the choice was my own, not made by the federal government. The stories of these women and others like them must be made available to Christians trying to shape their response to the abortion issue today.

Biblical Support

Some may ask why the discussion of biblical support for keeping abortion legal comes last, in Part 3. Shouldn't an examination of God's Word precede the stories?

As humans we learn from our experiences and those of

others. Thus God uses the method of story-telling to convey much of the truth of the Bible, limiting the dry discussion to short sections in between stories.

Furthermore, there has been too much arguing on the issue of abortion. "Pro-life" and "pro-choice" groups have their proofs clearly laid out—and Bible-believing Christians can be found on both sides. The Roman Catholic church opposes abortion, but Catholics for a Free Choice (CFCC) has materials to explain a very different Catholic position. Operation Rescue (OR) wants us to believe that all born-again Christians oppose abortion, but Evangelicals for Choice (EFC) exists and is growing. The mainline denominations have varying positions on a woman's right to choose, but the Religious Coalition for Reproductive Choice (RCRC—formerly the Religious Coalition for Abortion Rights) reminds legislators that most American Christians and Jews support choice.

For readers who would like to dig into the ethical debate, a summary of the main biblical principles supporting full procreative choice can be found in Part 3. A fuller discussion can be found in the pamphlets of RCRC, in *Conscience* (the journal of CFCC), or in books such as *Our Right To Choose: Toward a New Ethic of Abortion* by Beverly Wildung Harrison, professor of ethics and theology at Union Seminary in New York.[12]

For Christians who would like to move from intolerant argument to genuine dialogue on the abortion issue, a new organization has begun. The Common Ground Network for Life and Choice gives activists on both sides of the issue an opportunity to meet each other, talk about common goals and develop respect

---

[12]   Boston: Beacon Press, 1983.

for each other. The group's codirectors are Mary Jacksteit, a Presbyterian layperson, and Sister Adrienne Kaufmann, a Benediction nun. At dialogues held in several cities across the country in 1993, participants avoided labels and stereotypes for each other and learned that both sides shared a concern for reducing unwanted pregnancies. They began to focus on common enemies: ignorance, violence and discrimination.[13]

Myths and Persecution

Catholics for a Free Choice (CFCC) has a poster that says, "NOBODY WANTS TO HAVE AN ABORTION." In smaller print, the poster reads, "Picture a world where mothers have easy access to child-care they can afford. Where children can count on a good education no matter what school district they live in. Where people have health care whether or not they have a job. Where safe birth control is available to everyone who needs it. In this world, abortion isn't illegal. It's unheard of. Isn't that the best choice of all?"[14]

This poster is designed to dispel the myth that if you are not anti-abortion, you must be pro-abortion. In reality, no one is pro-abortion.

Another myth that needs to be challenged is the idea of "abortion on demand." No woman I have ever heard about has walked into a doctor's office and *demanded* an abortion. Many women have pleaded for an abortion, borrowed money, quietly

---

[13] "Abortion Activists Put Aside Rivalry," *Los Angeles Times* 12 Feb 1994, B4.

[14] "Nobody Wants To Have an Abortion," *Conscience: A Newsjournal of Prochoice Catholic Opinion* 14.1-2 (1993): 41.

signed papers for an abortion, or cried over the impossibility of finding anyone to do it. Some have cried over being forced into an abortion by their parents, boyfriend, husband, or—in some countries—their government. But the idea of a woman marching into an office like a cowboy in a western movie and demanding an abortion is far-fetched.

In fact, many women who have had an abortion have been unable to tell anyone about it. They have been unable to receive the most elementary kinds of human understanding and solace because they are surrounded by people who will only condemn them. Because of the continuing blame that their churches and society place on them, nearly all of the women in Part 1 have chosen to use a pseudonym. When I began this book, I expected that about half would use their own names while others would not feel able to do so, but talking with contributors and potential contributors enlightened me about the intense persecution these women face.

To present these stories even anonymously has taken tremendous courage. If their true names were attached, many of these women would lose their jobs in Christian schools and hospitals. Others would be tracked down by groups like Operation Rescue with its current emphasis on stalking and threatening anyone who stands up for women's choice.

The woman who is a pastor's wife does not want to jeopardize her husband's ministry. The pastor and the church counselor in Part 2 also wrote with pseudonyms, unable to come out in print with their pro-choice commitment based on family experiences and information gained in counseling sessions. Some pastors who have publicly supported legal access to abortion have encountered hateful mail, picketing of their homes, or posters of bloody fetuses placed on their churches by anti-abortion extremists.[15]

Increasing numbers of pastors, however, have taken steps to support full procreative choice. In Minnesota and North Dakota, nearly 100 clergy in eight denominations are part of a new Options Clergy Counseling Service. These pastors have been trained by the RCRC of Minnesota in how to offer nonjudgmental, reality-based counseling to women with unplanned pregnancies.

Christian women with such pregnancies often need spiritual counseling, something Planned Parenthood and other clinics do not provide. The Missouri RCRC has offered this kind of counseling on birth and parenting, birth and adoption, or termination of pregnancy since 1986. The Southern California RCRC recently began a "No Need To Hide Campaign" to connect people of faith with health workers in their community who provide abortions and need support.[16]

Stories Still Untold

In addition to the women using pseudonyms in this book, the stories of women who could not risk publication, even anonymously, would fill another entire book—and that book would be more heart-wrenching than this one. A friend of mine who had been adopted spent years searching for her birth mother. At one point during that period she found herself, a single woman, with an unplanned pregnancy. For her, ending the pregnancy was a

---

better option than giving up the child for adoption, because she knew from her own experience how abandoned and rootless that child could someday feel. One potential contributor is now a Marriage, Family and Child Counselor in a conservative community; in today's reactionary political climate, her practice could be jeopardized if her clients knew that she had an abortion early in her life.

In another very sad story a mother became pregnant against medical advice, trying to have a second child. She believed strongly in God's power to bring both her and her baby through a life-threatening pregnancy. Her husband, however, convinced her to have an abortion in an attempt to save her life, but she died six months later. If the pressure to bear children had not been so strong (internal pressure, social pressure, and church pressure to conform to an ideal of Christian motherhood), perhaps this young woman would not have begun a second pregnancy and might have lived to raise her first daughter.

In my work as a college English teacher, I sometimes find myself reading the papers of students who are recovering from experiences such as rape by a family member, childhood incest, sexual abuse by a priest, or date rape. Abortion is sometimes part of their story. I remember the student active in Campus Crusade for Christ who was strongly anti-abortion prior to her unplanned pregnancy. She decided to have an abortion (which was safe and legal—the year was 1980), but she was surrounded by so many people who opposed abortion that afterward she was still convinced abortion should be illegal.

Another student shared with me the experience of her aunt who after bearing six children found herself pregnant again in circumstances that to her were serious enough that she and her husband decided not to complete the pregnancy. A devout Catholic, she felt very guilty about this abortion and subsequently she bore four more children. But her mother, my student's grandmother, continues to reprimand this woman and call her a "murderer" because of this abortion that took place many years ago.

Of course, a factor in this story is the Catholic church's continued opposition to any form of birth control except rhythm and abstinence. A fertile married woman who obeys the teachings of the Catholic church really has no choice except to continue bearing children—unless she can convince her husband to agree to abstinence permanently or at least for part of every month.

I remember my own grandmother telling me how embarrassed she was to be pregnant for the fourth time in the first eight years of her marriage. In the 1920s, a woman obviously pregnant did not leave the house except when necessary. My grandmother described sitting at the window in tears, wishing she could get out and attend social events in the small town in which she lived. That pregnancy was her last one, so I was curious about what form of birth control she had used after that. Her answer was one word: "Abstinence."

I was shocked: a 60-year marriage had been a sexual relationship for only eight years. The love of my grandfather for his beautiful wife was legendary in our family, but my grandmother had also told me how lonely she had been as a young mother when he had stayed out late at night gambling or working at the store. Gradually I pieced together a picture of the strains on their relationship caused by my grandmother's determination not to be enslaved by any further pregnancies. The first two chapters in Part 2 include similar stories of women early in this century trying to balance fertility and the other demands on their lives.

The Legal Status of Abortion

The women who tell their stories in this book did not *want* an abortion. Raised as Catholics or Bible-believing Protestant Christians, most of them believed that abortion was not a morally acceptable choice—until each author found herself with an unexpected pregnancy that, if completed, would have had a devastating impact on her life. Under the grinding pressure of unique crises, these women made choices and eventually came to terms with those choices, changing their beliefs about whether abortion should be legal.

As Christians, we need to understand the difference between our personal choices about abortion and the legal status of abortion in society. Many Christians say, "I personally would not have an abortion, but I realize that abortion needs to be available legally in this country." These Christians comprehend that in a country made up of many kinds of people with different beliefs, abortion should be available to people who do not equate ending an early pregnancy with taking a human life. Such Christians also care about women who are desperate to end a pregnancy. They understand that these women will find a way to end a pregnancy, whether abortion is legal or not; keeping abortion available under safe and sanitary conditions saves these women's lives. Finally, insightful Christians realize that until I am faced with an unexpected pregnancy, and its unique circumstances, I do not *know* what choice I would make.

This book enables readers to see inside the lives of Christian women with unwanted pregnancies. Many who do so will conclude that abortion must remain a legal option—even though we all hope we will not have to exercise that option—and we hope that the abortion rate in the U.S. can be decreased.

We are agreed—both those who oppose full procreative choice and those who support it—that an abortion is a less-than-perfect solution in a difficult situation. We all want to reduce the number of abortions occurring in the United States today (about 1.5 million annually).[17] The question is how to do this.

Our disagreement comes in the methods we choose for reducing the number of abortions—and realistic observers say "reducing" because no method will ever totally eliminate all abortions. No laws or judicial decisions can prevent abortion; they can only cause a return to the illegal and unsafe abortions women have resorted to for thousands of years. Some possible methods of slowing the abortion rate are: improving birth control and the use of birth control, curtailing the emphasis on sexuality in our media and culture, providing support for women with unplanned pregnancies, and encouraging men to be more responsible about sex, birth control and children. These are the methods that pro-choice activists see as valuable in reducing the number of abortions. Christians who oppose abortion sometimes consider and use these methods, but more often they simply put their energy into making abortion illegal again—a method which might reduce but certainly would not stop abortion.

As a result of organized opposition to abortion and Supreme Court justice appointments during the Reagan-Bush era, the United States today does not guarantee all women full procreative choice. Women who live far from a metropolitan area, who are poor or who are under 18 are those most likely to encounter difficulty in trying to obtain an abortion.

---

17   Ann McDaniel, "The Future of Abortion" *Newsweek* 17 July 1989: 14.

Since 1977 the Hyde Amendment has allowed states to prevent women dependent on Medicaid from having an abortion option as part of their health care (unless the woman's life is in danger); as of 1992 only 12 states routinely provided Medicaid funding for abortions.[18] The Reproductive Health Equity Act currently in Congress is designed to insure that poor women will have equal access to full procreative choice. In 18 states a woman under 18 must notify one or both parents to get consent for an abortion; Becky Bell of Indiana is an example of a teenager who died in 1988 from an illegal abortion after her attempts to get a legal abortion without informing her parents failed.[19]

Women in rural areas have the hardest time obtaining abortions. The Supreme Court's *Webster* decision in 1989 allowed Missouri (and other states) to bar the use of public money, employees or hospitals for abortions. As a result, women in Missouri are dependent on a few private clinics for this procedure, and one clinic handles half of the abortions done each year in the state. In fact, 93% of rural counties in the U.S. have no abortion providers.[20] In Nebraska only two clinics exist, both in Omaha. As of 1992 North Dakota women have only the Fargo Women's Health Organization, and some must drive six to ten hours to reach this clinic. Individual doctors or clinics that perform abortions are required to have a hospital backup for emergencies, and hospitals operated by religious groups or dependent on state or federal funds can refuse backup services.

---

[18] Lacayo, "Abortion: The Future Is Already Here," 28.

[19] Mary Lou Greenberg, "Another American Tragedy: The Death of Becky Bell," *On the Issues* 17 Winter 1990:10.

[20] Irene Davall, "Which Way After *Webster?*" *On the Issues* 17 Winter 1990:9.

In 1992 another Supreme Court decision (*Planned Parenthood of Southeastern Pennsylvania* v. *Casey*) allowed states to require a 24-hour waiting period for abortions (thus a second lengthy trip for rural women).[21] Since the *Casey* decision, people who want to secure abortion rights have been directing their efforts toward legislation such as The Freedom of Choice Act and the Reproductive Health Equity Act. The addition of Justice Ruth Bader Ginsburg to the Supreme Court will help the struggle for procreative choice, but whatever its composition, the Court can only make rulings based on legislation and previous court decisions.

An Invitation

The purpose of this book is to present the realities of women's lives to Christians of all kinds—fundamental, evangelical, Spirit-filled, Catholic, Orthodox, Southern Baptist, Missouri-Synod Lutheran, Presbyterian, Methodist. These realities cause many Christians to work to keep abortion legal in the U.S. We are not asking those who disagree to change their position; we simply ask that you understand our position as another valid, Bible-based alternative. And we ask that you care about the women in your churches who need support when they face an unwanted pregnancy or when they hear self-righteous attacks from the pulpit on women who have "murdered their babies."

Yes, we would all like a world in which no abortions ever took place, but we live in a world in which birth control methods

---

[21] Rhonda Copelon, "What's Missing From the Abortion Debate," *Ms.* ns 3.2 (1992): 86. See also Eloise Salholz, "Abortion Angst: How the court's ruling will affect women, doctors, and activists on both sides," *Newsweek* 13 July 1992: 16-19.

sometimes fail and couples sometimes fail to use available birth control. Sexuality is flaunted and distorted in movies, on television, in advertisements and in the entire culture in which our children are raised. We live in a world where the crime of rape occurs every day—and many men who would never commit rape still expect to enjoy sexual intercourse without taking any responsibility for using birth control.

Once a child is conceived and born, too many men avoid full responsibility for its care or even its financial support. A woman who faces an unplanned pregnancy may have no emotional or financial support from her sexual partner or from her family. Because we live in this kind of world, some women are going to find themselves pregnant in circumstances that they judge to be completely unfavorable for the lives of the conceived children-to-be and completely unfavorable for their own lives. Women in this position who are desperate enough are going to have an abortion, whether it be safe and legal or unsafe and illegal.

Many Christians believe that the only caring response in this kind of a world is to insure that abortion be safe and legal. In fact, a recent newsletter of the Religious Coalition for Reproductive Choice notes that "the pro-choice movement was born in the religious community, born of horror at the reality of illegal abortions."[22] The most Christ-like approach is to keep abortion legal while also working to eliminate the problems that cause a woman to end the life she often would prefer to bear and nourish.

If you believe that abortion should not be legal, I ask you simply to read these stories and understand more deeply what

---

[22] "Bring the Word Home: Most Americans of Faith Are Pro-Choice," *RCAR Newsletter* 20.1 (1993): 2a.

you are asking when you require women to bear every conceived child, no matter what the circumstances. If you support full procreative choice for women, I hope this book will bring even more strength and courage to your convictions. If your thoughts are somewhere in between on the abortion issue, I encourage you to read these pages and think over what you find. If you have experienced an abortion in your own life, I pray that you may read these stories and find sisters who support you. May you enter further into God's grace and healing.

The women writing in this book have shared deeply of themselves. I pray that their lives and this book may continue to offer God greater glory.

Part 1

My Abortion §

1

The Baby I Could Not Give Away §

Heidi Vanderhorn

I met Gerry in Boston in the summer of 1974. We were students from a Christian university on a special mission to help people in the inner city. We lived in an old house on Park Street and each of us worked at a different place. I chose to work at a psychiatric hospital with children, and Gerry worked at a food bank.

My choice to work with disturbed children was the result of my job the previous summer. I had found myself caring for two unwanted children, and I needed to understand the problems I had encountered.

The two children belonged to a woman named Cindy who had three children, all with different fathers. These two were in the way of her plans to marry the father of the youngest, so she paid me to take them off her hands. Josh was five years old, a beautiful child but hard to manage. Julie was three. Cindy hit them a lot, especially Josh.

I had worried about Josh all the time. It was obvious Cindy loved her son, but she didn't know what to do with him. Once when I had taken the kids to Cindy's parents for dinner, Cindy's own father beat Josh in front of me. I hurried out the door with both kids, thanking their grandparents for the dinner and understanding why Cindy beat her kids. Whenever I met Cindy's relatives, they told me how Josh's father had committed suicide. Josh himself had heard it a thousand times, and he felt responsible for it.

That summer I spent weeks at the psychiatric hospital with children like Josh. There was Aaron, four, the size of a two-year-old; he had "acute failure to thrive" and scratched himself until he bled or banged his head on the floor. His mother had abandoned him in a bathtub when he was nine months old. Another memorable child was Stephen, also four, who had regressed to an infant because his parents took out all their frustrations on him.

Other stories like this abounded on the ward. Soon I became convinced that one must be mature and able to care for oneself before trying to care for a child. To these people, with so many personal problems, a baby was a burden, not a blessing. Their children might as well have been born into a country of famine and starvation.

After I returned from the psychiatric hospital, dragging myself off the bus, I found myself stopping in Gerry's small basement room to sit in tranquility amid his posters, religious books, and other things in sparse order.

He was quiet, shy and intelligent. I would come uninvited and tell him about the children until dinner time. I learned a lot that summer. My heart was full of compassion and a desire to help— as was the heart of every student on that mission.

In the fall I returned to the university for my last semester before graduation. What a total contrast it was to the inner city. Everyone was polite and said "Praise the Lord" a lot. All the cars tended to have bumper stickers with the Christian symbol of the fish.

The year before I had appreciated being with so many Christians, but after my inner-city experiences in the summer, returning took some adjusting. Our gracious life seemed somehow unreal. I went to the chapel often and prayed for the suffering children and all the traumatized people I had met who were trying to survive.

It was an emotional time for me as I reflected on life in the inner city and faced my future after graduation. Soon I started to write poetry and joined a poetry group, and there was Gerry.

I thought his poetry was sensitive and thoughtful. We started spending our free time together, writing poems for each other, helping each other with our verse. We became closest friends. Other students envied us because we had spent the summer in the real world and could write about things like bums and slums firsthand.

In December I graduated with plans to go to UCLA for graduate school. Gerry was staying on to finish his senior year. The week after finals I packed up to go home. We were saying goodbye. As tragically romantic youths, we thought the world was ending. We made love and I got pregnant.

In the shock and confusion, Gerry became like a stranger to me. He insisted that I have an abortion. I wasn't sure. Should I pay for my sin by having this baby? Gerry was so afraid it would ruin his life that I began to hate him for not caring about mine. I needed more time to think.

When I was back at my father's house, Gerry phoned me daily with advice, "You can't have a baby. You're so screwed up yourself that you'll ruin the child's life."

His words scared me. I had come from a broken home, and dealing with Josh and the other traumatized kids in the hospital had been difficult for me.

At night I tried to imagine what I could do for my child when it came. I looked at fetuses in books and learned that the one inside me was only a few centimeters and had no formed organs. It didn't seem as if it would be a murder, but Christian people said that it would be. Trying to guarantee the "rightness" of my decision, I decided not to have an abortion.

Threats kept coming from Gerry, however, so eventually I made an appointment for an abortion. When I called Gerry to tell him, I found out he'd shot himself and was in the hospital. Immediately the parallel to five-year-old Josh came to mind. I could hear people saying, "You know, Josh's father killed himself."

I thought of my poor baby. I also thought of poor Gerry, and I let him know that he didn't need to worry. I would have an abortion.

As soon as I hung up the phone, I felt as if a weight had lifted. Gerry was out of my life, and I suddenly realized he was out of the decision-making process. He couldn't hurt me any more with his cruel phone calls. I could rethink things. I canceled the appointment for the abortion.

By the fifth month of my pregnancy, my father and stepmother still hadn't figured it out, but they were worried because I was depressed. I slept a lot and was getting fat; I couldn't find a job. When I finally broke down and told them, they told me to go away as soon as possible. They didn't want family and friends, especially at church, to know about the pregnancy. I didn't want to be alone and I didn't have anyone else. "Where should I go?"

I turned to a home for unwed mothers. I realized that maybe I could go there and wait for my baby to be born. I found that I had to apply for state money (AFDC) to be accepted, so I did all the paperwork and soon moved into a fifth-floor linoleum bedroom with twin iron beds.

My roommate Lucy was a chubby 14-year-old who spoke in a little girl's voice and put pictures of kittens on the wall. She was the daughter of Baptist missionaries in Chile who had sent her away to give up her baby. They told her they didn't want their Christian witness to be ruined.

During the next two months I got to know all 28 girls, whose ages were from 12 to 17 years old. Some were Catholic, some Protestant, but all had chosen not to have abortions because they had heard Christians call abortion "murder." We didn't want to be called murderers, even if we didn't necessarily believe we were. Especially we didn't want our churches, which we believed in and needed, to condemn us as murderers.

Somehow I knew I had advantages the others did not and I felt such sorrow for the other young girls in that home with their lonely and traumatic lives. Most of them would live in poverty until they died because they had chosen to complete their unfortunate pregnancies and keep their babies. Many would never marry. Some would end up abusing or neglecting their children.

A few, like me, would give up the babies we carried, hoping for better lives for them. We loved our babies. We made baby clothes to send with them; we wrote poems and letters to them explaining our decisions, so they would not feel unwanted. In the end, we just hoped we wouldn't lose our minds, but in the end, we did.

When I was in my seventh month, I was told my father had suffered a heart attack and was hospitalized. Even though we weren't together, I felt he was all I had. The home, however, wouldn't let me go see him; there were certain rules the young girls had to follow, and this was one of them. I had to make a choice. I went to visit my dad anyway, but when I came back, I was asked to leave.

I arranged to move to a boarding house near the house on Park Street. When I arrived ready to move in, I was told the room was no longer available. I sobbed uncontrollably. The manager was rejecting me because I was so obviously pregnant. Pulling myself together, I looked in the yellow pages and went to three other places. Over the phone they all said that they had rooms, but when I arrived, either the rooms had just been rented or the price had doubled. No one would rent to a pregnant single woman. On my monthly $340 AFDC stipend, I needed to find a room and meals.

Finally I found the Vernon Hotel. It was a pretty place. The man behind the reception desk was soft-spoken and kind. He showed me all around. There was a double room with a shared bath for $320, and he said they wouldn't put anyone in with me unless the hotel filled up, which it rarely did. Because I was wearing a big coat, I thought maybe he did not realize I was pregnant. Unable to stand another rejection, I blurted out, "You know, I'm seven months pregnant."

"Congratulations!" he said.

I moved into Room 316 and Bobby, the gentle desk clerk of this cheap hotel, became a friend. During those last two months of pregnancy I made plans for my baby. I had decided to give the baby up for adoption partly because of my self-doubts about being a good mother and partly because of Gerry.

If I kept the baby, he would haunt us. How stable was he? What if he really did kill himself? I thought of Josh and his father's suicide. I couldn't risk letting my child be hurt like that. Perhaps most important of all, I knew how hard it had been for me to come from a broken home, and I wanted my baby to have a mommy and a daddy who loved each other.

Throughout my short life I had never felt closer to God than during those months carrying my baby. I spent hours praying and talking over my concerns with God. I spent a lot of effort asking God to help find the right family for the baby. I also told God how wonderful it was to have a precious life inside of me.

I believed this and did everything I possibly could to protect the baby. I gave up drinking coffee, swallowed horse pills for vitamins and even tried to keep myself cheerful in my terrible loneliness because I thought somehow that if I was sad or cried, the baby might feel it and be sorrowful too.

I found a lawyer who specialized in adoption. After telling him I wanted letters from people who wanted to adopt, I received hundreds.

Every day I would open my mail and tell Bobby, the desk clerk, what the letters said and what my concerns were. He didn't mind listening. He was kind and looked out for me. Though I was living among drug dealers and alcoholics, he wouldn't even let a person swear in front of me. After a while, everyone at the hotel began to like me and care about me. I felt protected.

Their kindness and concern were a drastic contrast from the cold reception I had from my Christian friends, who said things like, ''It's not my fault you got pregnant,'' and ''I can't do anything for you.'' Though some of these Christians were involved in projects to help the less fortunate, they somehow seemed convinced they were God's favored, in better standing, than the people they tried to help. A few explained to me that my circumstances and pain were my punishment for having gotten pregnant.

In spite of all this, God was with me and kept very close to me in my time of need, and eventually I found a good Christian family to whom I wanted to give my baby. Because I would have raised the baby in a church, I decided I wanted adoptive parents who would do this.

The baby came eventually. The happiest day and the saddest day of my life were one and the same; I was full of joy at giving birth, but sad to tear this piece of myself away. My father came to visit me in the hospital and said, ''Your mother and I will die someday, but that will not hurt you as much as this.'' He was right. He had loved me and he knew that I loved my baby.

After the nurse came and took my daughter from my arms, I stood for a long time with my arms out in the same position as when I had been holding her. I couldn't put them down. I was out of breath as if I had been punched in the stomach. When the nurse came back, I was still holding my arms out and staring at them. Straining to speak, I could only gasp out one word: ''Empty.''

The next few days were like a bad dream. I didn't eat. I walked around in a stupor. People who knew me said I was in shock. I was merely existing in an empty shell going through the motions of my life.

Somehow I moved out of the hotel and back with my father. I spent most of my days in my room overcome with grief. Legally I could have taken my daughter back, but I loved her and wanted better for her, no matter what it cost me.

I couldn't eat solid food and dropped in six weeks from the 150 pounds I had weighed before my daughter's birth to 95 pounds. No one could comfort me and no one really tried. My father asked me not to talk about it.

Feeling terribly alone, one day I decided to go back to the Vernon Hotel to talk to Bobby; I felt sure that he would listen. We had lunch and he asked me about everything. I told him how much I hurt. We had dinner together that evening and he was present with me in my grief. I began to see him every day, and I called him on the phone late at night and cried. I always cried. He would listen for hours.

Late at night was the worst. If Bobby and I had dinner together and I had to drive myself home, I would get into a terrible state during the 40-minute drive out to the town my father lived in. Bobby started driving me home in my car and taking the two-hour bus ride back to Boston. I spent all my time with him. One night, just as it had happened with Gerry, I did the unforgivable. Afterward I was inconsolable. In spite of all my efforts to be good, I had done it again.

At my six-week check up, my doctor had asked me what I was going to do about birth control. I told him then that I didn't need any birth control because I didn't believe in sex before marriage, and I wasn't going to make the same mistake twice.

Yet three months after the painful ordeal of giving up my child, I was pregnant again. What could I do? I was an emotional pulp over the loss of my baby. I was hanging on by a thread. At that point I couldn't carry another baby under any circumstances.

All through my pregnancy I felt proud of myself for not having taken "the easy way out." I believed I had done the right thing, and I clung to my rightness like a drowning person to a life preserver.

Now, however, I saw that my choice had been made out of fear. I was like the person who becomes a Christian because of a fear of hell. My choice had been governed by my fear of being called a murderer or being alienated from the members of my church—as well as fear that an abortion could not be forgiven by God.

During that pregnancy I had talked with God; I had listened for direction. As a result, this time I had the courage to rely on the spirit of God in my heart and not on doctrine alone. It came to me that the doctrine I had accepted on abortion was as provable—from either side—as other doctrines good Christians disagree over like baptism and what will happen in the end times.

I recalled words from the opening of Paul's second letter to Timothy: "For God hath not given us the spirit of fear; but of power, and of love, and of a sound mind." Instead of relying on my church's views on abortion, I decided to rely on "the spirit of power and of love and of a sound mind" that God had given me.

I imagined the few centimeters of life inside of me with no formed organs. If I didn't interfere, this life would become a person, but right now it wasn't like the baby I had already lost. I felt foolish for having clung so hard to my "rightness."

God was saying to me that I, Heidi Vanderhorn, was valuable and could choose my life. I could protect myself. I learned what it is like to let go of the last shred of self-righteousness—what we think earns God's favor—and instead just to accept God's love. In doing so, I realized that if I had learned earlier that *I* was valuable, I might not have gotten pregnant.

I also recalled the story of the time when Jesus told a man to follow him, but he replied, "First let me go and bury my father" (Mt 8:21-22). Burying his father was his way of being "right"—all good people were supposed to see to the burial of their parents. It was a duty this man thought would earn him righteousness, so he didn't follow Jesus. Trying to do the right thing made him wrong.

Trying to be right is a trap that springs from our pride. It usually keeps us from love and it clouds what Jesus taught. People may argue about abortion, but no one has the right answer. We have only our convictions. God knows our soul-searching, our honesty. God also knows when we judge and when we hate.

I had an abortion, and God was with me as much on that table as earlier on the delivery table. If you love me, you won't call me a murderer. You'll try to understand the horror of being pregnant when you don't have the resources or emotional strength to have a child.

For me, carrying a baby nine months and then giving it up is too horrible to recommend to another person. I might as well suggest that she burn her eyes out with branding irons, drink ammonia and sleep on razor blades—because that pain could not hurt as much.

Choosing an abortion, for me, was choosing life. It was, in fact, the first time I had ever acted as if my life mattered. Traditionally in this country, we have not condemned as murderers those who kill other men, women and children in wars. We call what they do "defense of the homeland" (and in our military history it's rarely been that).

What I did, I feel no guilt for. I only feel sadness that I didn't learn to value myself earlier and prepare myself for the kinds of things that happen in life. Had I only known that it's not a sin to take care of yourself, I would not have had to make regrettable choices about two pregnancies that could have been prevented in the first place.

2

That Terrible Night §

Barbara Hernandez

That terrible night will haunt me for the rest of my life. On March 19, 1989, I went to San Antonio, Texas, on a business trip for a child development workshop. At the time I was a student at the University of Texas at Austin.

My married sister lived in San Antonio, so I decided to stay with her for the weekend. Arriving at her house, however, I found she had suddenly gone to my parents' home for the weekend. Only my brother-in-law was there, so I changed my mind. I would only stay overnight. I knew the workshop would finish late, and I didn't want to drive back to Austin alone at night.

When I got to my sister's after the child development meetings I was tired, but I decided to prepare dinner for my brother-in-law and me. After eating, I sat in the living room for a while watching television. My brother-in-law, Joe, thought I was bored and asked if there was any place I would like to go for a drink or dancing. I was very tired and decided to stay home. He still went out.

Later that night, while I was in bed asleep, I heard a noise. Someone was opening the front door. Automatically I realized it was Joe, so I didn't get up to check, and fell back to sleep. I then heard the noise again. My bedroom door was opening and someone's tall shadow was standing there. I saw it was just Joe, so I relaxed, thinking he was getting something from the closet. Then I realized that he was approaching the bed. In that instant my eyes flew open and my heart started pumping fast. I was scared and confused about what he was up to. I asked him what was wrong. He answered that he wanted to be in bed with me. I could not believe my ears, but as soon as I realized what he had said, I jumped out of the bed and went toward the bedroom door. Before I reached it, he grabbed me and pushed me harshly on the bed.

I was frightened, screaming and crying and hoping some neighbor would hear my screams and come to help me. No one heard. Meanwhile my brother-in-law was struggling to take my clothes off. Because I was fighting back so hard, I was using up all my strength. I was kicking and hitting him and trying to get away, but he was so strong that nothing was successful. Still I kept fighting him back, but it made him more ferocious; he pushed me harder on the bed and took advantage of me. Joe attacked me sexually. I felt terrible—I just wanted to die.

When he was done, with the little strength I had left, I dragged myself out of the bed and ran into the bathroom and locked myself in. I was so frightened that I didn't want to come out and ended up staying there until I heard no noise in the house.

Finally I crept out cautiously, making sure Joe was not around. In the bedroom I got dressed as fast as I could and ran out of the house so quickly I fell down the steps. I drove off and stopped at the nearest phone booth to call my brother. Because I was crying so hard, he could hardly understand me. I managed to get the story out. It took a few moments for him to absorb the shock. When he finally found his voice, I could feel his anger towards Joe as well as his sorrow for me.

The night was beginning to fade into dawn and I still had to drive back to Austin. On my way back I kept getting flashbacks to the terror of that night. A few minutes after I reached my apartment, my brother arrived. He took me to the doctor and also took care of all the legal procedures for our brother-in-law to be punished for what he had done. He also informed my parents and my sister that I had been raped and by whom. What had happened was so hard and painful for everyone in my family to believe. Everyone felt anger and hatred toward Joe and concern about me.

I stayed in shock for several weeks, not only because of what had happened but also because of the doctor's later report. In the initial exam the doctor had performed a complete physical. I had been torn and bruised during the attack, but she wasn't sure whether I would have any long-term problems. When I returned to her office a few weeks later, she did another physical exam. This time the results were terrifying: I was pregnant. My heart stopped when she told me the news.

What a difficult position I was in. I had to make a decision on whether I was going to go through with this pregnancy. I was scared and confused because I believed that abortion was an immoral act, a sin. In fact, having been a Catholic all my life, I saw abortion as murder. I had not given the issue much thought, yet suddenly I had to decide whether I myself was to have an abortion.

Because of the circumstances of my rape, the doctor was totally against my continuing the pregnancy. She explained to me that in these circumstances I did not have to feel guilty if I chose an abortion. She presented it as a way to save my life, my sanity. It would not be murder. She was very clear that by no means should I go through with the pregnancy. She said that if I did, there would be chances of my not living a normal life because the flashbacks from my terrible experience would continue. Finally a joint decision was made by the doctor, my parents and me—and an abortion was performed.

At first I felt guilty. I had ended a life that was just beginning. But gradually I realized that because of my circumstances, it was better for both the embryo and me.

I now believe that abortion is a decision that may come from a woman's unique set of circumstances. It is certainly the best solution in a case of rape or serious deformity. In my situation it was the answer. This is why the legal status of abortion must remain as it is. Because of my experience, I support the laws permitting abortion. It is up to the woman to evaluate her circumstances and determine whether she is to continue her pregnancy or terminate it. I had to make that decision.

3

Abortion: Then & Now —
My Own & My Daughter's §

Wanda Payne

Twice abortions have touched my life. The first was mine 27 years ago. The second was my daughter's five years ago. The differences between our experiences are striking.

- Jennifer's abortion was done by a doctor; mine was done by a nurse.

- Jennifer went to a clinic; I went to an upstairs bedroom of a house without an address.

- I was with her before and after the abortion. No one accompanied me.

- It took Jennifer a day to recuperate from her abortion. It took me months.

- If she had complications, further medical care was available. If I had complications, I could have died.

- She had an abortion because she cared about her life, finishing college and becoming a teacher. I had an abortion because I was so ashamed that I no longer cared whether I lived

39

or died.

These differences are simply explained: hers was legal, mine was not. In the '60s to be pregnant and unmarried gave society a license to mistreat you. Parents could throw you out of the house and friends could abandon you. If your sexual partner married you, perhaps you were treated a little better, but you were still soiled goods.

Now young girls who get pregnant can decide to have an abortion without involving their friends or family. They can choose whom to tell and whom not to tell. Though there still may be some people picketing outside the abortion clinic, a woman doesn't have to break the law to have an abortion. If abortions are made illegal, society will begin to punish and mistreat women—again.

While more than two decades separated our decisions, both my daughter and I chose abortion as a means of resolving an unwanted pregnancy. I made this choice because I no longer cared about my life. In those days it was an anathema to be a young woman who had not "saved herself for marriage." There was no public school sex education, however, and certainly no access to contraception without parental approval.

Girls who got pregnant disappeared from the nation's high schools—spirited off to an unwed mothers' home or to the altar to be married in order to "give the child a name." Getting pregnant was a young girl's worst fear, even though many of us were not sure how it happened. (For a while I believed French kissing could get you pregnant.) What we learned, we picked up from our friends—and their sources were a mystery.

It was in this milieu that I succumbed to the promises of a young man, Bob, who said he would love me forever and wanted nothing more than to marry me. He was in the Marines, scheduled to go to Vietnam, so marriage would have to wait. For months he had talked about making love to me and wrote me long passionate letters—which kept me wondering what it would be like to make love to him. Bob explained that even though it was against our religion, it would somehow be right for us to do it because we were in love.

The night I finally didn't stop him, he had a sudden change of heart. Afterwards he told me he never wanted to see me again. "Any girl who would do that" he couldn't love. I remember him saying, "I'm funny that way." I was crushed.

Becoming pregnant never occurred to me because I had been told you couldn't get pregnant the first time you had sex. Wrong. When I finally told Bob I was pregnant, instead of keeping it quiet, he announced it at a party. As the news spread, my friends disappeared. I felt totally abandoned.

For my daughter, however, it was different. Jennifer and Jim had been going together for a long time before I began to suspect they were having sex. When I asked her, Jennifer hesitated a moment and decided to tell me the truth. When I asked what kind of birth control she was using, she told me, "Withdrawal and rhythm."

"Jennifer, that's not birth control. That's luck," I responded. I made an appointment for her and Jim to see a woman gynecologist. Jim sheepishly agreed to go. The doctor spent an hour with them discussing sex, reproduction and birth control. After that Jennifer began taking the pill, which made me feel more secure. However, she and Jim had a stormy relationship, and after numerous fights they broke up. Jennifer stopped taking the pill, but soon they got back together. After their reunion, she became pregnant.

When she told me the news, her words touched my core. Another unwanted pregnancy had entered my life, this time through my daughter. I wrapped Jennifer in my arms and told her that I loved her. Her younger sister, Cari, said, "See, I told you Mom wouldn't be mad."

The three of us—Jennifer, Cari and I—went to lunch and had a family meeting about what to do. Jennifer said Jim would go along with anything she decided. I thought, "Bless him." About to begin her junior year of college, Jennifer wasn't sure what she wanted to do. I told her she could have the baby (either keeping it or giving it to a family who wanted a baby) or she could have an abortion. The only thing I didn't want her to do was to marry Jim.

While Jim had his good qualities, he was very unstable and filled with rage, which came out when he drank. Once when he was drunk I had seen him smack Jennifer in the mouth and smash his windshield because she tried to keep him from driving. I believed they cared for each other, but I didn't want to see Jennifer legally bound to Jim.

After a lengthy conversation, Jennifer decided to have an abortion. I called a clinic in Pittsburgh and made her appointment. When the day came, I drove her to the clinic feeling thankful that I could be with her and remembering the time years before when I had felt like a criminal for getting an abortion.

Arriving at the clinic, however, we encountered a group of people who were trying to make my daughter feel like a criminal. Inside, waiting for my daughter, I realized how untrue is the claim that young women have abortions on whim. The mood in that waiting room was somber. Almost no one broke the silence. Looking into the eyes of those women, I could tell that each was contemplating her decision—and each was taking it seriously.

A few months later my daughter finally broke up with Jim. He couldn't handle it and shot himself. When he didn't die from that, he ran his car into a telephone pole and was killed. Jennifer has felt a lot of guilt and confusion about his death, but I have never heard her say she was sorry she didn't have his baby.

As a result of my own experiences and those of others I know and love, I feel strongly about women having the right to safe, legal abortions. Before it was legalized, many women literally risked their lives to end a pregnancy. Others learned how cruel society could be to unwed mothers.

When I told my father I was pregnant, he looked at me as if I had told him I had murdered my sister. "I'm glad your mother isn't alive to see this" was his first reaction. My mother had died of cancer four years earlier, and he explained that since he couldn't put his new wife through this shame, I would have to go live with someone else. "Maybe your aunt would take you," he suggested.

He put the house up for sale—the home where I had grown up in Canonsburg, Pennsylvania, just around the corner from a huge gothic Presbyterian church I used to attend with my two older brothers. He placed my younger sister in a boarding school 100 miles away to protect her from my reputation and stopped talking to me for months.

The shame was intense. At church I no longer felt welcome, the church which used to feel like the warm arms of my grandmother hugging me hard and long. The scene of many happy moments from my childhood had now become a place where people shunned me.

A few years earlier I had gone to youth group on Sundays, youth club on Wednesdays and had taught a fifth-grade Sunday school class once a month, as well as vacation Bible school in the summer. But after my mother died, I began to ask the Sunday school teachers and youth leaders some of the hard questions of faith. Her death changed the way I looked at God. How could God let my mother die when we all needed her so much? What had I done to deserve that? Had I not tried to be good?

Since being good didn't work, I went searching for something to fill the empty places in my life. My confusion led me from being a model daughter to becoming an outcast in my family. The neighbors stopped asking me to baby-sit and wouldn't even say hello. My friends weren't my friends any more. Only Sue stood by me. I went to stay with her family, who opened their home to me.

I had no idea where to begin picking up the pieces of my life. When I decided to have an illegal abortion, I wasn't scared for my life; in fact, I secretly hoped I would die. That would have been easier than having to live through the rest of my life without the love of my father and the support of my friends.

On the day of my abortion I arranged to meet someone in the parking lot of a church miles away. That person would drive me off to an unknown destination. As I waited, I looked at the old graveyard beside the church and realized that I could soon be there or in a place like it. With this resigned attitude I endured the lonely ride and soon found myself lying on the floor of an upstairs bedroom on a sheet while a woman (presumably a nurse) inserted a rubber tube into my uterus.

She told me to take some quinine pills and stay active—exercise—until the pain got so bad I couldn't stand it. Within a day or so, she said, I would abort the fetus. Then she left me there in the care of a man and woman I didn't know. I had washed down almost all the walls in their house before I finally expelled the fetus—in the toilet. I felt no love, no remorse—only relief. Then I went back to Sue's house and cried.

Again, 24 years later, the first thing Jennifer did when we walked out of the clinic was to cry. She said she was glad it was over and resolved "never again." Her words echoed my feelings as she cried, "Mom, I could never go through that again."

When my abortion was over, I claimed it had been a false pregnancy. Somehow that made me more socially acceptable. People began to talk to me again because they could pretend the pregnancy had never existed—and because half of my friends had sexual experience. Obviously my crime was not having sex, but becoming pregnant and forcing the community to deal with the reality of teenage sexuality and pregnancy.

The most painful aspect of the whole ordeal was that I was never allowed to talk about the abortion—how I felt or why I had decided to have one. Because no one would hear my pain or my questions, those suppressed emotions soon emerged in the form of actions to feel better about myself. Within a year I had married and was pregnant again with daughter Jennifer.

Time has passed, and with it has come much healing. Central to recovery was learning to separate the world's condemnation from God's. In God's natural order, the Creator—through biology—gave custody of all children-in-the-making to women, who alone decide whether or not to complete a pregnancy once begun. Had God wanted others to decide, God could have established some other biological process, such as laying eggs, to permit others to share responsibility for a child-in-the-making.

Furthermore, we draw our first breath at birth. Only then can we be baptized into our faith. In Scripture the words *breath, life* and *spirit* are used interchangeably. Equating a fertilized egg to human life has no basis in the Bible. In some ways, the anti-abortion movement seems closer to pagan beliefs than to Jesus' teachings. The pagans worshipped fertility and glorified the symbols of reproduction, much like the anti-abortionists today, who hold the capacity for life in higher esteem than life itself.

One lasting benefit from my abortion was that it made me empathetic and tender towards the outcast. I will never forget how it feels to internalize all the negative things that are said. Through the prophets and through the life and words of Jesus, God calls us to work for justice. My abortion prepared me to do that. I know I am to be an advocate for those who are discounted and put down. No one should cause another person to feel worthless. We all live under grace. And God always meets us where we are—not where we ought to be.

4

From Guilt to Grace:
A Long Road §

Christine Wilson

The weekend before Memorial Day of 1965 was much like any other, and I was much like any other middle-class 16-year-old. Except that during that weekend, in the space of five unplanned-and-not-particularly-earth-shattering minutes, I had sex for the first time and got pregnant.

My boyfriend and I were both virgins, good students, and involved at our schools in suburban Baltimore. We had been seeing each other for over a year. I was an active member of my local Presbyterian church and a sometime attendant at Young Life activities. Ricky was Episcopalian, and I sometimes went to services with him at his rather liberal church. I was particularly enchanted with the outdoor communion services they sometimes held, passing around a whole loaf of bread and a cup of wine, hearing from a rather young and bearded priest with a sweatshirt under his vestments. My Presbyterian tradition of stale white bread cubes and grape juice paled in comparison.

I don't think either of our parents really talked to us about sex. In my rather intellectual but shy-about-such-things family, we had several medical encyclopedias that we were encouraged to read. I also remember how shocked my mother was when I discovered the novel *Forever Amber*. Maybe as the only daughter (I had an older brother and two younger ones), the rules of the house were to protect me. For instance, I was not allowed to go out with anyone more than a year older. I knew a lot, or so I thought, about the technical side of sex. Ricky had tried to convince me once before it finally happened, but I had protested sufficiently that he had desisted. On that fateful day, we had gone down to the eastern shore of Chesapeake Bay to my parents' beach house. With no more impediments than bathing suits, passion overcame sense and in a few minutes it was done.

I remember feeling a distinct sense of disappointment (with which I did not wound my boyfriend's ego) before the fear of pregnancy hit me. I knew the consequences of the act. All of a sudden my calendar sprang into my head. It was the 15th day of my cycle, hardly an even close-to-safe time to have embarked on this experiment. To my embarrassment now, I tried the only thing I could think of and attempted to douche under the bathtub spigot (which, had I known, probably just speeded conception along). We took refuge in that common teenage rationale: "It couldn't happen to me," along with that other master stroke of illogic: "It was only the first time. ... " So, not knowing what else to do, we did nothing.

When a month came and went, but my period didn't, I allowed myself to believe that it was nerves. In 1969 birth control was not even talked about among my friends, and abortion was only an abstraction. In Maryland abortion wasn't even legal so far as I knew. There were no Planned Parenthood clinics with

women doctors; there was only my mother's gynecologist/
obstetrician, who had delivered my younger brothers and given
me my first Pap test not too long before.

I think I tried calling him once, but I couldn't get through the
nurse—a rather stern woman who intimidated me though maybe
she didn't mean to. I couldn't tell her I thought I was pregnant.
Besides, I might be overheard on the phone.

By July I was starting to fill out considerably, but through
dint of strenuous dieting I managed to look, at least at first, as
though I had finally started to "fill out." Ricky told me I didn't
look any different. When we went by airplane to his family's
summer home and I vomited on landing, we ignored the other
possible reason for my nausea; when I experienced seasickness
on our fishing outing, we continued to disregard reality. By this
time I thought it was too late to worry about it, so I tried not to
think about it.

School came, and I auditioned and won a part in a play.
When measured for my costume, I was relieved to find I had
basically gained three inches everywhere, so I bought bigger
clothes for school and tried not to puff and pant as I led dance
and kick steps for the drill team dance squad that performed at
the football games. And I turned 17. I got tired and missed
school more frequently. My mother became suspicious and one
day out of the blue she asked me outright, "Christine, are you
pregnant?" Not wanting actually to lie, I replied, "Mother!" in
an outraged tone. Either she didn't expect me to be pregnant or
she didn't want to know. At any rate, she didn't pursue it.

The time came when I couldn't fool myself any more. At
about the normal stage, I started feeling the life within me. I
would cry myself to sleep at night with my hand over my stomach, feeling the little occasional kicks, thinking how wonderful

this all would be in another place and time, wishing it were a bad dream from which I could awake. As I considered what to do, the stigma and shame of being pregnant at my school were all too vivid for me. I recalled the whispers and slurs cast at the older sister of a good friend of mine who had "had to get married" the year before. I don't think the school let her stay through the end of her pregnancy.

I had vaguely decided that at the latest possible moment I would run away to my grandmother in Arizona, have the baby there, and come back afterward. I rejected as a refuge my other grandmother in Missouri, a strict Congregationalist. Mostly I floated along trying not to gain weight and keeping busy at school. I stopped attending Young Life, though.

The day after Halloween reality came crashing down. I had stayed home from school with a stomach ache, and my mother called our family doctor. In those days they still made house calls. I remember lying on the couch, not meeting his eyes as he gently manipulated my abdomen, talking about constipation. He told my mother that there were certainly some "lumps" there and that I should have an enema. It was too much. When my mother came back into the room after seeing him to the door and started to say something about the enema, I exploded and said that I didn't want an enema and I didn't need an enema.

"Mother," I finally cried, "those lumps are bones!" which of course she didn't understand, so I laid it out for her (and for the first time said it out loud for myself): "Mother, I'm pregnant! I'm five months pregnant!" The rest of the conversation I don't remember. It didn't take long to convince her it was true. Then we both cried. We were both frightened of what my father would say. He was out of town on business as he so often was.

I told my mother my plan of going out to stay with Grandma to have the baby. We enlarged it with the idea of telling the school that I had tested poorly on tuberculosis or some other respiratory-type ailment so that I needed to be in the dry air of Arizona for a few months. My mother called my father at his meeting in Chicago, and he flew home the next day. Ironically, at this meeting of executives, someone had raised the topic of what they would do if they found out that their daughters had gotten pregnant.

When I told Ricky that my mother knew, he finally believed for the first time that I was pregnant. He cried then because he was afraid of having to tell his parents. Suddenly I felt older than he and coldly told him not to say anything to them. After my father got home, he asked me if I wanted to marry Ricky. I told him emphatically that I did not. My father met with Ricky separately. Neither one told me about their conversation except that Ricky had promised my father that we would not have sexual relations again. I was relieved. I had never really wanted to after that first time anyway. It only made me feel worse, and I didn't enjoy it. Ricky was also instructed that he was not to tell his parents as they would only think badly of me.

It was my father who brought up the idea of the abortion. I thought it was only possible in the first eight to twelve weeks of pregnancy although I had no idea of how to obtain one. He called someone from the Clergy Counseling Service, and I went to see a minister who tried to determine whether I wanted an abortion. I was so afraid and felt so guilty that I hardly know what we talked about. I was also embarrassed because the minister was the father of one of my friends (though not a close one) from school, and I was convinced that he thought I was a horrible person for what I had done. My father was afraid that

I would ruin my chances for college if I had the baby, even under my plan, as it would require my going away for so long. College interview time was approaching, and I was aiming at being one of the first women at Princeton or Yale.

I also went with my mother to the gynecologist to have an examination. I remember her telling me sharply to stand up straight as I walked. "I don't show yet," I answered, but she said that in a gynecologist's office I looked pregnant. The doctor was very nice and non-condemning, but he did ask me why I hadn't called him right after the weekend, when he could have given me a "morning after" pill. I told him that I hadn't known they existed. My mother had informed him about the proposed abortion, so he tried to reassure me that it would not affect my ability to have children later.

Three days after my father came back from Chicago, he and I were flying to London so I could have an abortion, if it were not too late by the time I got there. At that time, the only places we knew where it was legal to have a second trimester abortion were England and Japan. During the flight my father explained that the only legal grounds for an abortion at this late stage of pregnancy were the mental or physical health of the mother. Therefore, he told me, he was going to tell the psychiatrist I had threatened to kill myself because I was so overwrought at the thought of having this baby. "You must convince the doctor of that," he told me—which left me very uncomfortable since it wasn't true.

We got to London—it was my first trip—and we stayed in a nice, traditionally British hotel. It all seemed unreal—riding around London in cabs and seeing sights I could never tell anyone about. There was only one friend to whom I had been able to confide my pregnancy. Her nonjudgmental support, even when I told her about the abortion on the eve of my departure, was something that sustained me. Due to her Catholic upbringing, she would not have made the choice I did, but she continued to offer me understanding and acceptance.

The morning after we arrived in London, we had the interviews with the two doctors I was required to see. Despite my father's warnings about the legal requirements, I could not bring myself to be very acquiescent to his statements to the psychiatrist about my threatening to kill myself. Then I had to see the psychiatrist alone, and his scorn was apparent in the tone of the scathing questions he posed to me: "Didn't you know that if you had sexual intercourse, you could become pregnant? Why didn't you do something about this sooner?" I had to see another male doctor to determine whether the fetus was viable—in which case I would have made the trip for nothing. That doctor was matter-of-fact and not unkind, but I was still shaken from my interview with the psychiatrist, whose test I had apparently passed.

That night my father delivered me to the private nursing home where the abortion was to be performed. It was an old private home converted to medical use, and the uniforms of the nurses reminded me of nuns for some reason. When my father had gone, I was frightened at being left alone. The nurses took me to a ward of 20 beds filled with young girls, most of whom seemed not to speak English. Some of them had already had their operations. A few moaned occasionally.

I was examined and shaved in another room and given a hospital gown. After guiding me back to the ward, the nurse told me she was giving me something to make me sleep. Later I discovered (though it was not explained beforehand) that I had also been given a drug to dilate my cervix. In a few hours I woke in pain and began to cry. I was afraid and felt so alone.

A nurse came to my bed and started to tell me that there was nothing to fear and that I was fortunate because the doctor who was to perform my operation was very skillful and took his time. He preferred to make a small incision (apparently it was similar to a Caesarean section), and thus the pain I would have afterward would be much less than that of some of the other girls who were moaning in their beds around me.

Soon the doctor himself came in to see me and discussed the procedure, explaining that I was not going to have an abdominal incision at all. That was why I had been given the drug to dilate my cervix. He was going to do what he called "something like a D & C" vaginally. I tried not to focus on the fact that he was basically talking about going inside me and cutting the baby into pieces so he could get it out. This remains for me the most difficult part of my abortion to think and talk about; it still makes me wince. I tried to view it as he appeared to, concentrating on my relief at not having to undergo major surgery. He said that my body would be much less affected so that after I healed, not even a doctor would be able to tell that I had undergone an abortion. With some difficulty I managed to get back to sleep. Soon I was wakened for the operation in what appeared to be the middle of the night.

In the operating room, the doctor and the anesthesiologist did not say much. I remember asking with some difficulty if they would tell me if it were a girl or a boy. The doctor either said he wouldn't tell me or that he wouldn't be able to tell; I'm not sure now which he said, but he did not seem happy to be asked. Then they gave me some kind of gas through a mask.

The next thing I knew, I woke up in a private room and my sheets were soaked with blood. A nurse changed them, changed me, and told me that my father was there to see me. I was still in a haze from the anesthetic and literally saw him as through a pink cloud. I felt so happy and relieved that he was there, but I wasn't coherent. I recuperated for another day and a girl from Germany, only 16, came to share my room before her abortion. I felt so much older. She was as frightened as I had been; I felt sorry for her, but because of the language barrier, I was powerless to reassure her.

The next day I was released, and my father took me sightseeing. I remember how scared he was when I almost fell down the steps of the Tower of London. I was too weak for much exertion, so I rested the remaining time until we flew home. Our story for my missing school was that I had been away on college interviews and had taken ill.

Afterward my father and I didn't talk much about the abortion. In fact, on the way home from the airport he said that unless I wanted to discuss it, he would never bring it up. For years I felt *he* didn't want to talk about it—perhaps because he was ashamed of it or of me or because he was angry at having to deal with the problem and pay for all the expenses involved. It took me almost 20 years to raise the subject with him; finally I realized then that he might not have meant it that way at all.

In those days before abortion clinics, after-counseling was unavailable. Fortunately I had the one friend in whom I had confided, and later at college I had a few roommates to whom I could talk about it. (As it turned out, I didn't make it into the Ivy League school that I wanted, partly because I was still an emotional wreck when the time for my interview came.) The result of those confidences was strange: among those few friends, I became someone they could turn to years later when a couple of them got pregnant and had legal, early abortions. I remember telling them that I couldn't really be helpful because it had been so different for me. I don't think any of them told their parents, though, so at least I was someone they could talk to.

Without any counseling, I felt a lot of guilt that I could not expunge, so I tried denying it. When abortion rights became a political issue, I was quick to defend the right to choose when to have a baby. Abortion became legal in New York, and other states' laws were challenged. Whenever I was dating a man, I told him about my abortion early in the relationship, factually at least, fearing rejection and wanting him to know about it sooner rather than later. In college I became somewhat of an agnostic, as well as a typical liberal, hippie, flower child of the late 60s, though East-coast rather than California-style. I stopped going to church though I sang in the college choir, which toured local churches.

Before graduation I married a classmate and went through a traditional Presbyterian wedding ceremony in my home church. Mother admitted that she had told our minister about my abortion, and he had been sympathetic, not condemning. This response surprised me because of his office, though it fit with what I knew of him personally.

After ten years of marriage, having finished law school and then working as an attorney for two years, I was ready and eager to have a child. I was relieved to get pregnant right away because secretly I had feared that I might be punished by having difficulty when I wanted to have a baby. When my son was born, I worked part-time during the first couple of years, unable to bring myself to leave him with a sitter all day. I also thought about the baby I had not had. It really hit me each year when it came to the time of year that I thought she or he would have been born. For some reason I always thought of that baby as a girl though maybe it was because my husband and I had a son.

When Kevin was two, I started thinking about church, being drawn back to it. We joined the local Presbyterian church and became actively involved. It was a Bible-based church, and although the minister and the congregation were friendly and warm, there was a conservative political atmosphere. Soon after we became members, the minister held a forum on abortion. No one else who attended the session questioned his extreme opposition to abortion—except me.

This experience prodded me to start reading the Bible and other theological sources to see if my pro-choice position was un-Biblical. It was a scary project, but I really wanted to answer the question of whether abortion could be a valid choice for Christians. An added difficulty was my being a lawyer: I needed to deal with the issue by separating the legal questions from the spiritual ones—yet doing so made me feel split.

When I turned 34, it struck me that the baby I had aborted would now have been the age I was when I made that decision. This fact affected me strongly because at the time I was involved with the youth of the church and had become close to many of the girls. That year I was asked to teach a group of preteens. One of the things the youth director and I would cover in these meetings was values relating to sexuality. Intuitively I knew the abortion issue would be raised, and I had to think seriously about how to respond. When the class met, the minister's daughter had the guts to ask the youth director what he would tell a young high school girl if she got pregnant. I was upset that his answer was absolute: her only alternative was to have the baby. Though I didn't want to get into an argument, I felt obligated to point out that the Bible did not expressly prohibit abortion—as far as I could tell after reading a number of biblical commentaries on the subject. I also drew on what I knew of the Presbyterian church's official statement on the complexity and difficulty of the decision, but I really couldn't articulate the church's position too well. I was simply defending the process of deciding between two or more undesirable outcomes, not defending abortion itself as a good in itself.

During this same period, along with becoming more active politically on the issue of abortion rights, I also discovered Christian feminism. A door opened into a whole new world for me as I read feminist theology and finally found other women who supported the notion that "Christian feminist" was not a contradiction in terms. Our local ecumenical study and support group became a haven for me to discuss abortion and other issues from a Christian perspective, as well as the Bible from a feminist perspective.

The concept of women being moral agents equal to men became the linchpin that held together my Christian beliefs and my belief that reproductive choice must remain a legal option. I no longer felt split between my spiritual convictions and my legal understanding.

My spiritual understanding now strengthened my beliefs as a lawyer on the Constitutional issue. It became simple, in fact. Women must have the right to make their own decisions, even those they might later come to regard as mistakes. I no longer had to try to justify my abortion as the least wrong of several bad alternatives, as I had so often done in the past. Regardless of my particular decision, the importance of women's moral agency makes legalized abortion not only appropriate but necessary from a Christian perspective.

I don't deny the pain and grief and the strong need of forgiveness that I had over the years. I prayed and asked forgiveness of God, Jesus and the baby; I even thought of tracking down Ricky for his forgiveness, but some barriers remained in my forgiving him—his not being there for me and his insistence at the time that it was all my fault. Last year, however, out of the blue he flew into town on business and called me. We went to dinner and talked about his wife and her daughter from a previous marriage, whom he helped raise. He never had children of his own and never wanted babies. Without our even talking about our past relationship, somehow a lot of healing took place.

Meanwhile my political activism has expanded to preventing teenage pregnancy, not merely protecting the right to abortion. I wouldn't want anyone to go through what I endured. In some ways my experience looks so easy: my parents not only knew about it but arranged for the abortion and paid for it. During the years when I was in denial, I too said that mine was one of the easy ones, before I began to realize its full impact.

It is difficult for me to describe the searching—and all the tears—involved in getting close in recent years to a complete resolution of my abortion experience. Too much else has been happening at the same time: the dissolution of my marriage after almost 15 years, the resolution of my mother's place in heaven despite her suicide when I was 23 years old, and my finding a Mother (even more than a Father) in my God. These factors make it difficult to isolate the process of coming to terms with my abortion; each is another story in itself.

Someday I would like to put all these pieces together and see the whole picture, but for now I know one thing for sure: abortion must remain legal and accessible. By beginning to parent and nurture the wounded child inside me, with God's help and guidance, I have gone through another stage of healing of my abortion experience—without consciously trying to at all. I no longer struggle with whether the decision to have the abortion was truly mine or my father's. I know I would have made the choice early in that first pregnancy if I had access to a safe, legal abortion.

Therefore, along with caring for my son and working as an attorney, I devote some of my time to the effort to keep abortion legal and to guarantee other girls and women access to the information and services they may need. If I had such access in 1969, I know it would not have taken 25 years to attain the peace of mind I have today.

5

Mother of Two — Not Four §

Katherine Emery

I remember the joy of that Christmas vacation and the freedom to enjoy my life, including sex with my husband, now that I was free from that unwanted pregnancy.

In the fall of 1971 my husband was in his third year of graduate school in Gainesville, Florida. I was supporting us both by teaching remedial math in high school. This was my second high school teaching job and though it was difficult, I was no longer crying every Sunday night because I had to go back to teaching Monday morning.

Matthew and I had been married for a year, and I had been taking birth control pills. What I read, however, indicated that long-term use was not recommended, so I was trying a new intrauterine device, the Dalkon shield, which was supposedly easy to use for women who had not given birth.

My first period after beginning with this IUD never came. I saw a doctor and spent a miserable Thanksgiving, sick from the progesterone that would bring my period if I were not pregnant. It didn't work; I was pregnant.

Both Matthew and I knew that having a child at this point in our lives would be a disaster. I had seen the gyrations my fellow teachers went through with child care. If I were healthy enough to stay at work until the birth of the baby, would I be able to continue teaching while nursing an infant? Would I be able to get the baby to child-care and still travel the 40 miles to school by eight each morning? Or would Matthew end up quitting graduate school to support us? I had hoped to be home with my children when we started a family. All we could think was that having a child at this point could ruin all our plans.

We knew that our minister at the United Church of Christ was connected to a local abortion referral service, so we went to him. While he regretted that we could not rejoice at our impending parenthood, he referred us to an Episcopal priest who did abortion counseling and who in turn referred us to a sympathetic doctor.

Because it was 1971, finding a doctor willing to help us could have been difficult. Later another friend told us how severely she had been castigated by a doctor whom she had picked randomly from a phone book. We realized how fortunate we had been in our own procedure.

The doctor concurred that I was indeed pregnant and that the IUD had settled so far down in the uterus that it could easily be pulled out—by hand. He had me do this since he couldn't risk being charged with abortion, should one result. Since abortion was then illegal in Florida, the doctor referred us to a clinic in New York City. Although in 1971 some twelve states had laws permitting abortions, only two—New York and California—did not require residency for women seeking abortions.

Calling the New York clinic, I made an appointment during the Christmas holidays when I would not be teaching. With my references, doctor's statement and plane ticket in hand, I was ready to wait until the holidays, but suddenly I received notice of selection for jury duty. When my first jury day came, I found a way to speak with the judge privately, explaining that I couldn't serve because of my scheduled abortion. The judge mentioned how lucky I was to be able to make these plans—abortion had only recently become legalized in New York—and he called me "Miss."

The day of my trip finally arrived. My biggest fear was that I would get too hungry and possibly lose consciousness. Pregnancy had increased my appetite, and I found myself getting faint if I went for several hours without eating. Because of the possibility of the use of anesthesia during the abortion, I had been instructed to eat no food after midnight. I worried about how vulnerable I would be if I became faint while walking through airports or trying to find my way through New York—a strange city that seemed dangerous to me.

Though I hadn't tested hypoglycemic, low blood sugar had affected me before and I had gotten sick from the combination of hunger and a disastrous snack of cookies. I decided the best solution was to eat a huge meal right before midnight and to pack a small suitcase full of healthy food to eat after the abortion. I also brought a slick woman's magazine to read, thinking that the other plane passengers would be mostly business travelers and that reading this would be a good cover-up for what I was really on my way to do.

The trip turned out to be difficult. Leaving from Jacksonville, about 80 miles from my home, I had to transfer planes in Atlanta, where heavy fog delayed us, nearly making me miss the connecting flight. Somehow I made it to New York in time. The recommended taxicab company gave me no hassle, and I arrived safely at the clinic.

My appointment began with a required counseling session, a time of reassurance that I had no doubts about whether I wanted an abortion. This also gave the counselor a chance to share her own story with me and comfort me with the knowledge that I wasn't alone. I explained how difficult it would be for us to care for a baby at this point in our lives, and I was thankful that the counselor provided gracious support in helping me to examine my own priorities.

Soon I got into the hospital gown and was assigned a bed. The doctor, an Italian-American, came in to examine me and explain the procedure. When he left, he gave my hand a warm squeeze that somehow soothed away some of the trepidation I felt at being exposed in this awkward position and in this unfamiliar setting. I was grateful for his warmth and surprised at how soon the procedure was over.

The anxiety of the past several weeks began to ease, and I was glad to note that I was not as faint from hunger as I had feared. As soon as I got to the recovery room, I opened my suitcase and ate the soup in my thermos and the other nourishing foods I had packed, along with the orange juice offered by the clinic.

After an hour of recovery and further instruction from a nurse on how to care for myself and watch for infection, I was allowed to get dressed and move to the lobby. I had to wait there another two hours for observation purposes. There I reassured a student from Africa that his girlfriend was receiving kind and gentle attention. I also told him that I had experienced my abortion positively, as a blessed release.

When I was allowed to leave, I faced the two remaining problems: trying to find a place to eat dinner cheaply and getting to the airport on time for my flight home. I have no memory of the cab, the airport or the plane ride back home except that the winter fog interfered with our plans. The plane had to land in Orlando, several hours south of Jacksonville, where my husband and our friends were waiting for the scheduled arrival a little before midnight. The airline sent us passengers by bus back to the Jacksonville airport, so the people who cared about me waited up most of the night.

The next day Matthew and I slept in. We reflected on the whole experience: trusting in a medical procedure that had failed to work, we had then chosen another medical procedure—expensive and far away—to cope with that failure. Then, to nurture ourselves after this ordeal, we went shopping and bought me an expensive pair of beautiful silver earrings. We also bought fuzzy fabric to make throw pillows for the plastic day-bed couch. What I remember most about that day is the glorious freedom to see, to hear, to touch, to take time.

As I look back now, having had two beautiful children and having invested myself full-time in their care, I still am in real doubt as to whether my marriage or my sanity could have survived an infant back in 1971. I am glad I had the opportunity to choose to have children when I was prepared to care for them. I now do home-schooling for both my children and am active in the California Home-Schooling Association. I simply could not have done these things for my children if they had come into our lives early in our marriage.

In fact, Matthew and I had to make another family-planning decision when our boys were toddlers and we discovered that another pregnancy had occurred, in spite of our efforts at birth control. This time, since we already had two healthy children requiring my attention, I was even more confident than before that we had made the right decision. We also took steps to limit the size of our family through permanent, surgical means of birth control.

Matthew and I enjoy singing together and performing in choral groups, especially around Christmas. We appreciate the increased amount of time and energy we have to be active in our church now that our children are older. And I am finding that some of the freedom I experienced during that Christmas season in 1971 is taking root in my life once again—the freedom to be who I am and to nurture the talents that God has given me.

6

Cracking Up —
Or Coping §

Elise Randall

It was a hot, humid summer day in 1976. I sat in the examining room, waiting for the doctor and wondering which was making me feel worse—the weather or the mild but persistent nausea that had dogged me for the past two weeks. In addition, I was irritated with the doctor for wanting to do a pelvic exam and a urinalysis. It should have been obvious that I had the flu. So what if my period was overdue? That wasn't unusual.

Just then the door opened. "Well," the doctor announced matter-of-factly as he reentered the room, "you're pregnant."

The lights bobbed and wove crazily. For a moment the room itself seemed to be spinning around me. I wanted to cry. This was news many people hoped and prayed for. Such news sent them scurrying off to make excited phone calls to relatives and to refinish garage-sale cribs. Christians especially were supposed to be overjoyed to learn a baby was on the way. (How often had

I heard Ps 127:3 quoted? "Children are a heritage from God, the fruit of the womb a reward.")

Yet for me, it wasn't that way at all. The doctor's announcement seemed like a bad, bad joke.

The preceding year had been enormously stressful for my husband and me. Despite our best efforts, we had ended up in a situation that was a personal and professional nightmare. Creative ways of redeeming the situation seemed almost nil. Staying put could only mean being dragged deeper and deeper into frustration and misery.

For months we had racked our brains, trying to plan a workable exit. At last we had hit upon a reasonable solution that entailed moving from Chicago to a city some distance away. We had already laid the groundwork for this transition and were looking forward to moving when I got the news.

Naturally, I was stunned. Me, *pregnant*? Somehow it didn't seem possible. Not that I questioned my reproductive capacities. It was just that a family was the last thing on our minds. We had pretty much assumed that we would have children when the time was right, but we hadn't been married all that long, and the time definitely *wasn't* right.

The more I thought about it, the angrier I got. I was angry at the doctor who had recommended a diaphragm when I could not tolerate birth control pills. Never had he warned me how unfoolproof it was. I was angry at friends who swallowed the pills almost like candy and didn't get sick *or* pregnant. But more than anything, I was furious at God for allowing this to happen to me. Was this my "reward" for the strain and unhappiness of the past year? Was I a person in God's eyes—or just a walking womb?

I thought of the millions of women throughout history who had undergone unwanted pregnancies, even dying on account of them. I reeled at the injustice of it all. I thought of the careful plans that would have to be scrapped if I went through with my own pregnancy. I felt cornered.

Providentially, my husband and I didn't have to face the dilemma completely alone. That very day some Christian friends from out of state arrived for a visit. They listened calmly as I poured out my anguish and perplexity. Finally they said, "We won't tell you what to do, but we do have something to suggest. Make a decision together; make it quickly; and then don't look back." A few days later they were gone, and we were left to agonize in private.

The week that followed was pure hell. I had never dreamed I might have to confront the abortion question personally; after all, I was married, not a teenager or a single woman. I was also an evangelical Christian, a graduate of Wheaton College. Yet here it was, staring me in the face.

The doctor said I was eight weeks pregnant. I could either arrange for an abortion very soon or I could expect, seven months down the road, to give birth to a child that neither my husband nor I was prepared to parent. It was that simple.

My husband was similarly wrought up. Like me, he had never expected to encounter this problem, let alone at this time. Nevertheless, he was prepared to see me opt for an abortion as an emergency birth control measure, and he was ready to respect my feelings either way.

Technically, it was our decision. But it was *I* who would be damned no matter what we decided. *I* was the one who would be called "murderer," "selfish," or "immoral" if anyone found out that I'd had an abortion. And *I* was the one who would be labeled "unloving" or "a bad mother" if I bore a child I wasn't prepared to cope with.

Where could we turn for help? The Bible seemed to be silent on the issue. Of course, there was the sixth commandment, but it only applied if what was developing inside me could be called a real person. I wasn't at all sure of that.

We could hardly turn to relatives for advice. They would be too outraged at the possibility of denying them a grandchild, niece or nephew to offer any real wisdom. We couldn't share our problem with the people at church. The pastor and his wife had just had their first child after years of infertility, and the congregation was largely composed of young families. Not to want a child right now would be incomprehensible to them. I could just hear their smooth assurances: "Everything will be fine!" "How *wonderful!*" "You'll be thrilled!"

I was quite certain that we *wouldn't* be thrilled. At best, I thought, we would grin and bear it. At worst, our lives would fall apart. I began thinking of Christian couples we had known in the past who had unplanned children. In almost every case, the marriage had been severely strained. Also, the women had borne the brunt of things. *They* were the ones whose working lives had been forcibly interrupted and to whom most of the child care had fallen. Most of them had been visibly unhappy, yet instead of being helped or regarded compassionately, they had been severely criticized for their shortcomings as mothers.

I was struck with the hypocrisy of churches that tune out such persons' anguish. These churches hang onto illusions about family life instead of grappling with unpleasant realities. They praise parenthood (especially motherhood), while steadfastly refusing to help those who aren't ready for it.

When I pictured myself as a parent, I didn't like what I saw. In our present circumstances in Chicago (where we would have to remain if we had a child), equal parenting would not be possible. Instead of going on to new challenges in my work, I would be trapped at home with a baby. I was filled with resentment and afraid that I might take out my frustrations on the child in ways that would do lasting emotional damage.

The twin possibilities of messing up an innocent child's life and seeing our own lives permanently altered—for the worse—by something we hadn't planned on, made abortion seem the logical alternative. However, the question remained: did we have any right to tamper with nature? Was it God's will for us to have a child regardless of the consequences?

In the midst of all this I found myself thumbing through Walter Trobisch's little book on contraception, *Please Help Me! Please Love Me!* What struck me was Trobisch's emphasis on the principle of dominion in Genesis 1:28 ("And God blessed them and ... said ..., 'Be fruitful and multiply, and fill the earth and subdue it; and have dominion over ... every living thing that moves upon the earth' "). Trobisch's claim that "letting nature take its course" might actually be an *evasion* of dominion, of responsibility, made me think long and hard. If that were true for contraception, why should it not apply to abortion? Might not the choice of an abortion in our case be more pleasing to God than bearing a child we were not equipped to deal with? Would preventing the emergence of one life be worse than truncating *three* lives?

These thoughts made sense to my husband as well. Although neither of us liked the idea of abortion, we had to conclude that it was the most responsible alternative for us at this time. With resoluteness, and yet with a certain sorrow, I phoned a women's clinic not far away.

A few days later, I had the abortion. It was by no means as easy or as painless as I had been led to think—a reminder, perhaps, that nature doesn't like to be interrupted. But the immediate result was an overwhelming sense of relief. Now we were free to deal with the existing problems in our lives instead of being crushed by new ones.

This is not to say that we have had no regrets. To the contrary, there was (and is even now) a definite feeling of loss. Eight years later under much happier circumstances we became parents by choice, and our ten-year-old daughter is a source of much joy and satisfaction for us. Nevertheless, we do wonder what might have been if we had been emotionally able to finish that first pregnancy—or what would have happened if I had not had the abortion and the situation had deteriorated. My husband feels that I would have miscarried from the sheer weight of emotional stress. I wonder whether our relationship would have cracked under the strain.

Only God knows what might have been. But I like to think that our decision was one in favor of dominion, a decision based on responsibility and discipleship.

7

A Pastor's Wife
Faces Truth   §

Claudia Davis

It is very difficult to write about my abortion experience. Almost 13 years have passed since that time, yet I still find it hard to put into words all of the emotions that come with the memories of that event.

Nonetheless, I want to share my story so that others will know that women don't get pregnant and have abortions because they want to. For me, it was an agonizing decision that I made when I was 27 and will live with for the rest of my life, as part of my history.

Although I never expected to be in a position to consider abortion, I learned that abortion does not happen in isolation. It is a personal decision that is made in the context of the circumstances of a woman's life at the time. And through it all, there is God.

I was raised in Oregon in a "loving, Christian home" that on the outside certainly looked normal to the rest of the world. My father is of German ancestry and fairly typical of the dominating, authoritarian male found in patriarchal religion. Our family went to a fundamental church where one's relationship to God was often based on fear and judgment. God's unconditional love and acceptance were not familiar concepts to those in my church, and certainly no one in our home ever talked about God in those terms.

When I was nine, I gave my life to Christ after a missionary had spoken at our church. There were loving, caring people in my church family—as in any church fellowship—but I also remember vividly the condemnation and fiery judgment heaped on those who were not following the right path.

At one point our evangelical church was merging throughout the country with a more mainline church (Methodist). Those very folks who had helped nurture me in my faith, the older ushers who had given me Hershey kisses on Sunday mornings as a young child, would stand up in anger and shout that they would not become Methodist—for Methodists were surely going to hell! Several churches in the northwest, including the one I grew up in, pulled out of the merger. Years later, wouldn't you know, I married one of those liberal United Methodist pastors— and I couldn't help but wonder if my old friends all thought I was going to hell.

Coming from that religious background, I often struggled with what it meant to be a woman. In the context of male domination, it took some effort for me to accept my own sexuality and realize that I am a person of worth. As I have matured in my faith—often being forced to do so through new experiences—I have come to a new relationship with God, who is both mother and father to me and so much more. I have come to sense the joy of all creation and the unconditional love of my

Creator.

Out of this context I came to the decision facing me in that fall of 1977. My husband and I had only been married three years, and we had just returned to Denver to complete his final year of seminary. The previous 15 months had been spent in Tucson, Arizona, where he served as an intern in a local church. During this time our first son was born, and his birth was a joyous occasion for us. The women of that church showered us with unending presents and attention. Many of the handmade gifts we received were from people we didn't even know who wanted to support this young couple during the birth of their first child.

When our son Ryan was seven months old, I had extensive jaw surgery. It was a terrible shock to wake out of an eight-hour operation, in which my mouth had been wired shut, and find my face discolored and swollen to the point that my husband could not recognize me. Bone had been taken from my hip to form a new upper jaw. The pain from the bone graft often felt worse than that from the jaw surgery itself.

For four weeks I remained wired shut and could hardly communicate, let alone eat. Everything I consumed had to be put in a plastic syringe and then squirted through my teeth. Some days just preparing enough thin soup to get adequate nourishment took all my strength. Strained tomato soup only goes so far! Sometimes the syringe would stick and I'd end up with soup down my front instead of in my mouth.

During this time I was dealing with being a first-time parent, going through the accompanying anxieties and sleepless nights, as well as recovering from my first major surgery. In addition, I had to stop nursing Ryan because I was taking so much medication. Day-to-day life was extremely stressful, and I lost a great deal of weight.

In the strain of this four weeks I began to suspect I was pregnant. When I went to my doctor, explaining that I felt many of the symptoms of being pregnant, he was shocked that I would be suggesting such a possibility so soon after Ryan's birth. He told me that he didn't think I was pregnant and sent me on my way.

Within the next few weeks we moved to Denver for Kyle's last year of seminary. I continued to feel pregnant. The move itself would have been traumatic enough, but along with it we had to deal with my surgical recovery plus all that goes into having a ten-month-old child whose schedule is being disrupted and whose surroundings are changing. Left behind were all of my extended family and the network of friends who were my support through the birth of our first child and through my surgery. Because of my weight loss and all the medications I had taken during this time, I was very concerned about long-lasting negative effects on the embryo if I were indeed pregnant.

Finally I went to take a pregnancy test, and this time it was positive. I will never forget standing in the seminary's student health clinic when the nurse gave me the results, thinking she was passing on marvelous news! In a daze I walked home, wondering how I was going to cope with another baby when I hardly had the energy to take care of myself.

It was my husband who suggested that we consider an abortion. I doubt whether I could ever have brought up the subject, though the possibility had occurred to me. Over the years I have wondered how much Kyle influenced my decision. I had only been married three years, and there was still a part of me that worshipped the ground he walked on; often I would play that submissive role I had been conditioned to play. In the environment in which I grew up, I was not used to having any control over my life. Consequently, I had a hard time making decisions or even knowing what I thought about things.

Kyle was engulfed in completing seminary—no easy task— and worried about supporting his family through the year. He had his own male issues to deal with. Having another child was the last thing on his agenda for that year.

My voice shaking, I finally called to get my appointment to talk to someone at Planned Parenthood. As it turned out, our counselor was a member of a United Methodist church. Later, as I continued to deal with my decision to have the abortion, it was comforting to reflect on that discussion with her, a Christian who could affirm me as a person and support me through a decision I never thought I would have to make.

The next days went by in a blur. Within a week I was sitting in the waiting room, moments away from my turn. I noticed several young girls there alone without a husband or family support and wondered how they would ever make it through. Though Kyle wasn't able to be in the waiting room with me, I felt his support.

The procedure itself was far more traumatic for me emotionally than physically. I remember the suction machine and some discussion about how far along I was. Because of our move to Denver, I was about twelve weeks pregnant by the time I had the abortion. Since then I have looked at pictures of a fetus at twelve to fourteen weeks and have wept over the loss of that potential life. It was not an easy decision. I had to wade through enormous grief before I could be at peace about ending this pregnancy.

After the abortion I went home to my young, energetic son and to the four walls of our small student apartment to contemplate my actions. The decision to end a pregnancy can feel tragic—filled with sadness, doubt, grief, and guilt—even if you believe it is the right decision. I had a lot of emotions to get in touch with. At first I was just numb to some of them, but I felt so much sadness at the loss of that potential life.

Part of my decision certainly had been based on the quality of life for that unborn child. I was far from recovered from major surgery and had not been able to eat proper nutrients during those crucial first months of pregnancy. No one could answer my questions about the effect on the fetus of the drugs I had been taking. Financially, emotionally and spiritually neither my husband nor I was able to offer the kind of love and care that we knew a newborn would need.

Much of my later work professionally has been with children and mothers struggling with domestic violence issues. In many families with whom I have counseled, violence has escalated during pregnancy. When there are children present in such homes, it seems especially heartbreaking; they and the mother may have no way out of a deadly situation.

When I consider the emotional costs as well as the cost to society of the various needs of children raised in such turmoil, I am convinced that abortion must remain a legal option. Children need a minimal level of quality of life. When they don't receive it, the result can be violent behavior as adults. Women who choose abortion think about what kind of life their child would have. Thus it grieves me when I hear people call us ''murderers,'' especially when they assume that we made our decision lightly with no regard for human life.

Although the judgments of people opposed to abortion were hard to bear, my husband and I carried on with our lives. No one else knew that I had ended a pregnancy. I regained my health. Kyle completed seminary and found a good job in Kansas. It was time to have another child, and I became pregnant.

Suddenly the debate over when life begins surfaced again in our lives: our second child died at full term. The baby had been fully formed and functioning before he was deprived of oxygen during delivery *(placenta abruptio)*. Moments later he was still-born and was not issued a death certificate.

It certainly seemed odd to me that his life did not warrant an official recognition of death—since so many people argue that life begins at conception. They would condemn me for ending the life of a fetus at three months, but legally a baby who lives until moments before birth is not considered enough of a person to have his birth and death recorded. At the time I did not pursue my questions any further, but someday I would like a legal interpretation.

We had the joy of the birth of another child, a son, two years after our baby died during delivery. I have always been thankful for the health of my children and the love and laughter they bring to our family. There have been times, however, when I reflect on having three boys and wonder whether the aborted fetus was the girl I had always wanted. Such thoughts are haunting.

I am not an advocate of abortion. Like marriage or raising children, abortion is something we get into without realizing the full impact and long-lasting effects of our decision. Nevertheless, I am an advocate of freedom of choice. When the conflicts of life come up, each woman must be able to answer for herself, with prayer and support from her family and religious community, the crucial question of whether to bear this child. The religious community must respect the rights of others and not impose its view as the only answer. God comes to each one of us as an individual and offers us salvation in a personal encounter. So be it with our religious journey.

The lonely secrecy surrounding my abortion was one of the most difficult parts of the whole experience. All the couples at seminary seemed to be fine, upstanding Christians. What would they think if our secret was out? Except for my husband, no one knew of my abortion, and for Kyle the experience had less impact than it did for me. It was difficult for him to understand what I was going through, and it was hard for me to communicate my confusion and doubt about our decision. Now I realize that I could perhaps have talked about the abortion with others and received support from them, but at the time I carried it deeply within. It was easier to have a guilt trip and not talk about it.

In the years since then, I have begun to share my experience—and I find that I am not alone, of course. In fact, by talking about it, I discovered that my sister-in-law and my best friend have both been there. When I was sharing with another pastor's wife about writing this chapter, I learned that she too had chosen to have an abortion. I know that many pastors' families guard secrets, trying to live up to the image of the perfect family.

Sometimes I hide things out of concern for jeopardizing my husband's job. "If they really knew the various crises we've gone through, Kyle would not get that church," I think. Or "This church would kick us out." Increasingly, however, I realize how important it is that we share our experiences and understand that we are not alone. We gain strength from understanding what we have in common in our journey as women.

When my husband and I lost our second son, I struggled with old messages left over from my childhood that God must be punishing me for my awful sin. My natural grief over losing the baby was magnified because the loss triggered my unresolved guilt over the abortion. To aggravate the situation, my husband was going through a major crisis in his life with his first church and had an affair with a close friend of mine. She even came to be with him when I was in the hospital with the dead baby.

After the trauma of discovering them together two months later, I went into a deep depression over the loss of almost everyone in my life who had been important to me. Again, as a pastor's wife, this is not something you can share with friends in the congregation. The loneliness I went through at this juncture was beyond description. I pray for the day when the walls will come down and pastors' spouses will be able to come together and share their pain, for it is out of that brokenness that God is present and can be glorified.

Through this experience I truly came to understand the grace of God, the art of forgiveness and reconciliation, and the ability to face overwhelming grief and survive. It has taken many years of diligent, difficult, determined work, but we have all come out of this ordeal with renewed faith in God. Each of us has experienced a sense of real forgiveness and the reality of God in our own life. Our history together became even more poignant when that same friend lost her ten-year-old son to cancer. Once more we struggled with those old beliefs that it might be God's punishment.

These later developments became an integral part of my journey toward accepting myself and the circumstances of life that I must deal with—including the abortion. All of these events brought me to a fuller understanding of God's presence in my life, no matter what comes my way. My journey toward interpreting and accepting my abortion experience became part of that larger picture. Through those combined experiences I gave up my idea of God as the one who punishes us for our constant mistakes. In reality, God gives us the strength to carry on when we are in the midst of tragedy and grief.

One of the miracles of this journey is the growing relationship I share with my husband. I went into the marriage expecting him to take care of me and be my knight in shining armor. Obviously, when he fell from that place of honor, he fell hard. There was no way we could return to a relationship in which I idealized him.

Some might be tempted to say that Kyle must not be much of a man of the cloth if he tolerates abortion and had an affair. My answer is this: Yes, it would be delightful to live in a perfect world with no unwanted pregnancies, no messy affairs, no suicides or poverty. But the fact remains that life is here to be lived out with all its ambiguities and often agonizing conflicts. God's patience with Abraham, Isaac, David, Saul and others certainly bears witness to the need to face reality, not just condemn it.

Kyle and I are sharing a life together today because of the grace of God that continues to enter our life, showing us how to embrace all that comes. We are far more emotionally healthy and realistic in our relationship. We have been able to use these experiences and face our humanness, even when we are broken and in pain. As a result, our witness is much stronger today. Our ministry, as individuals and as a couple, is much more sensitive to the realities facing those around us. God is able to use our personal stories in small ways every day.

For me and for many women, the hardest part of the abortion experience is the secrecy we feel compelled to keep because of the cruel words and behavior of many of those who oppose abortion, including Christians. I sometimes wonder how their personal experiences may have shaped their outlook on life.

Coming from my conservative religious background, I have some understanding of the exclusive mentality, the rigid world view, and the need to condemn others in order to maintain control of the flock. This atmosphere certainly doesn't allow for any questioning of the accepted, right way of doing things. Even though I understand these people in some ways, I am still repelled by their tactics—so condemning and intolerant of anyone else. How fragile their righteousness is when they must denounce others in order to make themselves feel pure.

One of the greatest tragedies of the church today is that we are not free to admit our pain and suffering and share our burdens. So often the church turns a deaf ear to the violence experienced by women and to the hurts that both men and women carry in this world. Often I have noticed that women like me who have come from fundamental, strongly religious backgrounds are more likely to suffer psychological trauma from abortion and to carry the emotional scars longer. Yet God is present to heal those wounds and offer us new life.

My reading of the New Testament makes it clear that the church of Jesus Christ is a place where people can go when they skin their knees or their hearts, where judges don't judge and each child of God is beautiful and precious. Peter and Paul demonstrated that it is a place where people can disagree and hold hands at the same time.

The church of Jesus Christ calls us to live responsively—not only on Sundays, but throughout the week when we are faced with agonizing decisions. In those hard places we are called as Christians to witness to God's love and forgiveness. To be faithful to our Savior, we must work toward reconciliation and understanding—not name-calling and condemnation—to solve our differences. Only as we begin to voice our pain and to let the secrets heal, are we able to journey into wholeness.

8

Pressure To Be Perfect §

Jo McIntosh

I come from a close-knit family of four daughters, two older than I and one younger. From birth our parents instilled in us the necessity of getting a well-rounded education so we would not have to be dependent on a man for our economic well-being. This education included religious training in a mainstream Protestant denomination: Sunday school and church, youth group meetings, vacation Bible school and summer camp. We grew up believing in God and knowing what to do and what not to do in order to please God.

Education was also important in our family because my father was the high school principal in a small Iowa town where I lived all of my school-aged life, playing with the same friends each year in a comfortable and well-established routine. But suddenly, at the end of my first year in high school, my parents announced we were moving. My father was going to be principal of another high school in a similar sized town an hour's drive away. This unexpected jolt in the continuity of my life was very upsetting. Outwardly I remained calm and did what was expected of me by my parents, but inwardly I felt desperately alone. That summer I got to know a few kids from our new church. Because I met them there, my family and I thought they were nice kids, appropriate friends.

In the fall when school started, I suddenly realized these new friends were totally different outside the church setting, but I was angry and rebellious enough over my upset life to follow my peers' lead. My new best friend, Carolyn, and I started going out together on the weekends to dances and parties. We drank, picked up men, and *definitely* stayed out past curfew.

During this sophomore year in high school, I dated a man for several weeks who eventually broke up with me because I would not sleep with him. He immediately started dating Carolyn, and a few months later she got pregnant with his child. She really struggled with what to do about this pregnancy. When I asked her, "What do you want from life? Will you be able to achieve that with a child?" she decided to have an abortion. Our group of friends supported Carolyn as much as possible and she seemed to be doing okay; everyone thought that she had made the best decision, considering where she was in her life. Carolyn continued to attend church and seemed to feel right with God.

We went through another summer having fun by going to the park, dances, movies and parties. Everything revolved around men and boys, who would get picked up, and who would pick someone else up. I turned 16 that summer and considered myself to be all grown up. Late in the summer, Carolyn and I found ourselves with serious boyfriends. I had begun dating Steve, and after a few weeks he and I started having sex.

Around Thanksgiving I realized I was pregnant. Steve and I had already talked about what would happen if I became pregnant. I made an appointment to have an abortion during my Christmas break. We did not tell either set of parents; we just did it. Steve drove me to the clinic and paid for everything.

Telling my parents about either my pregnancy or my choice to have an abortion was just not an option. As the high school principal's daughter, I felt I needed to be the perfect example for my schoolmates. If my parents knew, then everyone would know, and I was trying to protect my father from undue pain. In retrospect, I think my parents probably would have been accepting, but at the time I didn't think so. Even my three sisters never knew. To this day I have no idea whether they have ever been in a similar situation, but I think not.

The one person I confided in was Carolyn. I'll always remember telling her about my pregnancy and coming abortion. We were alone one night at my home taking care of a sick kitten, and I told her I was pregnant. We had a short conversation and she went home. But the next day when I got to school, I found out that she had been committed to a psychiatric ward just a couple of hours after I told her of my plans. Though she had seemed totally together and capable of helping me through my problems, she was in deep trouble herself. When I went to visit her in the hospital, Carolyn tried to talk me out of the abortion. She made me walk through the nursery and look at all of the newborn babies. I refused to take Carolyn's advice and had my own abortion. Carolyn stayed on the psychiatric ward of the hospital for a couple weeks and was then released.

I've never felt guilty about my abortion; it was the best decision for me at that time. I was 16, a junior in high school. How could I fulfill my parents' mandate of getting a college education if I had a child? How could I live up to my highest capabilities and God-given talents if I had a child before I had a chance to realize what those gifts were? How could I bring myself to give up a baby for adoption after carrying it for nine months? By that time, the child would have been too intertwined with my thoughts and emotions to give away easily.

Yet I will never be able to forget my pregnancy, my child. Even though I was only pregnant for ten weeks, I always know, in the back of my mind, that I would have had a little girl. I know how old she would have been right now, what grade in school, and all those things a mother just instinctively knows. But those thoughts are a small price to pay. I would have felt a lot worse bringing that baby into a life of poverty with few hopes and fewer dreams because I had no way of supporting her. How could I justify ruining both lives by giving birth to a baby I could not support? I freed the spirit of that child to enter another child who would have a better life, and I freed myself to be all that I possibly can be, maybe including a mother later in life.

I did feel incredibly guilty about my part of Carolyn's story. For several years I felt that my pregnancy and planned abortion were the complete cause of Carolyn's illness. Recently I have been able to realize at a deeper, emotional level that Carolyn's problems were just that: *Carolyn's* problems. If she could not handle my pregnancy, then that was her problem, not mine.

During those turbulent years I continued to attend church because my parents expected that of me. It never occurred to me to break the rules about church attendance. I broke all the other rules, but not this one. Something kept me in church, although I felt God had abandoned me. God seemed to be a remote white male who could do whatever he wanted and still be good, but he expected "good girls" to be totally pure in order to be acceptable. Now I realize that at some deeper, subconscious level God was working in my life. I had those painful teenage experiences for a reason; God understood that reason and did not let me leave the church while I was working through them. God kept a small flame of religious desire alive in me to let me know that even if no one else was there for me to lean on, God was.

Through God's grace, I graduated from high school and attended a small private college in Iowa, completing a double major in politics and religion. Then I worked in a church and community center for over a year. After that experience, I attended seminary in the Chicago area. At first I planned to become a pastor, but because of difficulties faced by women and minorities as ordained pastors, I switched from the master of divinity (M.Div.) program to the master of theological studies (M.T.S.) program—a non-ordination-track degree. I graduated in 1992 and am learning a great deal in the church where I am currently working.

In seminary I grew away from the white male image of God into other, more positive images. I have become more comfortable with myself, with God, and with what it means for me to be a Christian. Because of my continued relationship with God, I have come to feel forgiven for the mistakes of my life. I now see that during my 16th year, my mistake was *not* the abortion but my ignorance of how to use birth control properly. I thank God that I did not bring a child into an unhappy home with a mother who was unprepared to cope with raising a child. I also thank God that I had a choice—an opportunity to continue my life the way it was meant to be lived.

Carolyn and I have lost contact with each other. The last I heard, she was a practicing R.N., happily married and anxiously awaiting the birth of her first child. Steve and I dated five more years after the abortion. During the first three years he served in the army as a paratrooper; then he came back and started college. He never allowed his feelings about the abortion to show, but we broke up over entirely different issues shortly before he graduated from a two-year college.

Since then I have married and my husband and I are now considering when to start a family. Sometimes I reflect on the lives of Carolyn, Steve and me, all now in our mid-twenties and well-launched on our separate paths. I am happy that God gave the medical profession the ability to perform safe, legal abortions and gave us the intelligence to make thoughtful choices. The right answer for one person is sometimes the wrong one for someone else. Perhaps abortion was not right for Carolyn, but it was definitely what I needed to do at that particular time. I continue to ask God for the strength not to judge other people's decisions, just as I ask others not to judge mine. Only God should judge our actions, and each one of us must learn to make decisions that are appropriate for the circumstances.

Abortion is not right for everyone, but it *is* right for some people and those people should not be punished because others believe it is immoral. If we make abortion illegal on moral grounds, then many other personal choices could be declared illegal on moral grounds. As long as abortion is medically safe and as long as it does some good—as it did for me—then it should be kept legal.

9

Obeying My Husband, Giving Up My Child §

Joyce Owens

[Editor's note: Being pro-choice means supporting the choice to complete a pregnancy as well as the choice to end one. The following story is an example of an unplanned pregnancy that a woman wanted to continue but her partner wanted to terminate. If a woman is willing to take full responsibility for a baby, she should have the freedom to complete the pregnancy (see Part 3, "The Bible and Choice"). However, Joyce Owens found her church leaders allied with her husband against her choice to keep the baby. Their purpose was to save the marriage at any cost and preserve the ideal of female submission to the husband. Ironically, the church also opposed abortion and expected Joyce to have it done secretly and bear the emotional burden alone.]

What happens when two dearly held fundamentalist principles collide? I found out when I moved to rural New England after many years as a Baptist. Finding no Baptist churches nearby, I joined a large non-denominational body of

Christians whose goal was to build a New Testament-style church, focusing on community and total commitment of their lives to Christ. Being far away from the extended family in which I was raised, I was attracted by their focus on caring and sharing plus their sense of belonging, which I missed.

However, as a college professor training teachers of young children, I had been accustomed to assuming leadership roles and functioning independently. I soon discovered that independence was not possible in this church. Wives were to be subject to their husbands in everything, no exceptions.

No married woman was allowed to become a member of the church without her husband's permission. Unmarried women were under the headship, or control, of a male home group leader or elder, or they were required (if they did not live with their parents) to live in the family and under the headship of one of the men in the church. Women were not allowed to have any role of leadership or decision-making in the church. Members of the church took an active role in campaigning against the Equal Rights Amendment and against abortion.

My move to New England from Delaware had been prompted by a decision to protect myself and my five children from continual abuse by my husband, Tom. The separation was successful and life improved for my children and me, but five years after the move Tom and I were still in close contact. I had two children still living at home, the youngest eleven.

My new church put me under immense pressure to be reconciled with my husband. I resisted this for a while, but after Tom began taking medication for high blood pressure, his anger seemed to subside and he invited me to come back to Delaware to live with him.

With the encouragement of the church, I agreed to do this but since I was under contract as a college professor and reconciliation would require a move of several hundred miles, there were some months before I and the two remaining children could rejoin Tom. During that time he and I resumed intimate relations.

Then I became pregnant. We had not planned this, but I was enthusiastic about a new beginning, another chance to raise a child in a loving Christian atmosphere. We would do it right this time, I dreamed.

As a specialist in early childhood education, I had no job possibilities in the area of Tom's home, but we could well afford another child. I knew I would enjoy this rejuvenating challenge. My one-year-old grandson would have a baby aunt or uncle to play with and, after all, I was only 41 years old. I was also buoyed because Tom had recently said he might go to church with us this time around.

As I shared my news with Tom, sitting in a cozy restaurant overlooking Lake Champlain, I was full of thanksgiving to God for this blessing on our reconciliation. I was totally unprepared for his dismay. "But it's so impractical," he kept repeating. Unable to convince me with any of his reasoning, Tom kept insisting that I must have an abortion. "It's the only sensible thing to do," he stressed.

We finished that meal and the weekend of his visit without any resolution to our differences on this pregnancy. At the time I could not understand his opposition to having another child.

After returning to Delaware, Tom continued to call and insist I must have an abortion. Finally he declared that I could not move back with him until I had had the abortion.

I was devastated. Not only had I resigned my teaching position, leaving me unable to provide for myself and the children if a reconciliation did not work out, but all my hopes and dreams were being shattered. I thought of the expectations of all my friends at church, who were so delighted at how "God had saved another marriage." How could I tell them how high the price would be?

I sought out a trusted elder and explained my dilemma to him. What should I do? I asked him if he would intervene on my behalf with my husband.

After conferring with the other male leaders in the church, he came back with his response. The male leadership agreed it would not be good for me to have the pressures of an additional child while trying to resume a marriage. But the most important issue was that I must obey my husband's decision.

The church did not approve of abortion and believed that I would be committing a grave sin if I had one; nevertheless, my husband's authority was absolute and none of them would speak to him about changing his mind. The only help they offered was to pray that Tom of his own accord might decide to allow me to keep the baby.

That change of mind did not happen, so the day came for my abortion. One of the elders and his wife dropped me off at the corner of the street where the abortion clinic was located. It was obvious that they did not want to be seen anywhere nearby. "We're going shopping and we'll meet you for lunch at the diner on the corner," they said, quickly disappearing.

Slowly I walked the half block to the upstairs clinic on a busy city street. "How could I think of food, after going through this?" I wanted to ask them.

Inside it didn't seem at all like a medical space; there were lots of posters and literature for various causes in which I had no interest. The young woman assigned to be my counselor asked me why I wanted an abortion, and I told her how I was learning to be a submissive wife and how my husband had to learn to assume responsibility for his leadership.

She didn't understand any of this talk and especially not any of my tears. I kept clutching my New Testament and praying for the miracle deliverance that was supposed to save my baby and me from this trial.

As I returned to the waiting room, I noticed that nearly everyone else had someone with her to stay by her side during the waiting period and then take her home afterwards. I had only my New Testament. "Though I walk through the valley of the shadow of death, I will fear no evil. ... Lord, forgive them, for they know not what they do. ... Wives, be subject to your husbands in *everything*. ... "

I kept repeating verses over and over to myself, interspersed with prayers for deliverance: "Lord, you honored Sarah's faithfulness in obedience to her husband when he sold her off to a harem. I beg you to intervene miraculously on my behalf, too. ... God, as Abraham was called upon to sacrifice his dearly beloved son, I offer this baby up to you in obedience. Where is your substitutionary ram? Even now you can deliver my baby as you did with Isaac."

But there was to be no miraculous intervention, only the sound of my sobs, with no one there to hug me or wipe away my tears. The doctor's assistant proceeded with the abortion. I tried to close my eyes so that I could at least mentally escape, but the attendant said I had to keep my eyes open "to make sure I was all right."

Afterwards I was sent to lie down in a recovery room with several other women. Between sobs, I noticed that every other woman in the room had someone else there with her offering her comfort and support.

I opened my Bible to Psalm 27: "When my mother and my father forsake me, then the Lord will take me up." I prayed, "O Lord, I need you to take me and comfort me now."

An hour later the elder and his wife picked me up at the diner and took me home. No one else in the church was informed about what I had done.

I called my only sister looking for support. She was very sad but explained to me how much Satan loves it when he can back Christians into a corner so that whichever choice they make, it will be a sin.

This was not much comfort.

A non-Christian friend in whom I confided invited me to spend a few days recovering physically and mentally at her home by the lake. It was peaceful and refreshing there, and she let me just be, without pressure to talk. I felt that I had offered up my baby as a sacrifice for my husband's salvation. I still couldn't understand why God had not intervened, as in the story of Abraham and Isaac. I had been so sure that deliverance would come. My trust in my husband, my family, my church and my God had been crushed.

When I returned to church the next week, one of the women there questioned the appropriateness of my having left my two teenagers alone at home for three days while I was at the lake. I knew I couldn't tell her about my need to recuperate, but it was too late to matter anyway. I went through the motions of living, as in a fog. When my children and I moved back to Delaware, the illusions of the people in the church remained intact:

I was going off into the sunset with another healed marriage for which they could praise God.

I dutifully went off with my two children to try to begin a new life with Tom. When I shared the abortion experience with him, needing support for the loss I had experienced, he wondered aloud whether that child had even been his and then refused to discuss the subject ever again. For nine months we lived together although Tom was very remote and uninvolved with me and the children.

Then suddenly, like a whirlwind, the "reconciliation" was all over. We were spending a quiet summer vacation in the New England town I had moved away from, enjoying the company of our older married children, who all lived nearby. The mountains and the fresh air were a welcome change.

Tom and I went out in our sailboat, and out on the lake away from the children he dropped his bombshell. He abruptly announced that he did not want me to return with him to our home. The explanation was shattering: he had begun a relationship with another woman during our separation and he had continued it during our supposed reconciliation. He was not ready to break this other relationship off, and he could not stand the tension of maintaining a sham marriage.

The illusion was over. There I was, back in the church where this had all begun, full of pain and sadness, silently confronting the members and elders with the complexity of real life. I had followed their rules for God's will and I had even had the abortion my husband required, but it had not saved my marriage.

I wish I could say that my experiences had some impact on my church, in causing them either to allow women more say in their lives or to accept the legal status of abortion. Unfortunately, however, most people did not know about the abortion.

In fact, the elder who had taken me to the clinic became very distant and aloof, as if to deny his awareness and his responsibility.

The shame rested on me alone. I was viewed as a failure in my attempted reconciliation with my husband. (No one knew about Tom's lover; they knew only that I had failed to please my husband.) The number one rule for women's subordination was never examined, regardless of the pain and death that were its price. This church continues to speak against the situation ethics of liberals and non-Christians, contrasting it with an ethics based on the inerrant truth of the Bible. Nevertheless, in actual situations not clearly covered in the Bible, fundamental Christians like these rely on a sort of working code that defies logic and ignores God's concern for persons.

The emotional price paid by me and my children during this period in our lives was tremendous. Moving twice, going through the pregnancy and abortion and being without a job amounted to a series of catastrophes. Because I was overqualified for most employment opportunities, we lived in poverty for two years. But the greatest pain was in not finding any loving support from Christians as we went through these trials. Instead we found hypocrisy.

In retrospect, with the wisdom of another decade of living, with a better grasp of the truth of Scripture and with my growth in knowing God, my decision would be very different. I now have the freedom of being in a more responsive and responsible Christian community, and I have a support system of other women who have been set free by the real Truth. If I were now placed in a similar dilemma (though realistically it is now impossible for me to conceive), I would choose to have the baby and sacrifice the pretense of marriage.

The Lord has blessed me with a granddaughter born to one of my daughters during the same week that my baby had been due. Susanna has been very special to me, a joy in my life. She just turned eleven and I gave her first brassiere; we shared a precious time of celebration of womanhood. I'm trying to teach her to respect herself and her body and to safeguard her ability to make responsible choices—in a way that I wish I had known sooner.

My abortion experience and subsequent events were instrumental in my decision to leave that fundamentalist church and to research for myself what the Bible has to say about women. Through this oppressive ordeal, I discovered that what I was hearing and being taught about God did not coincide with what I felt at a deep, inexpressible level about God's love and God's acceptance of persons.

I was delighted to find that women theologians and biblical scholars had been working on these issues for years; their work was available in Christian bookstores, but not the ones I had been going to. Thank God for the liberation I have experienced since then and for the growth in my self-esteem and my involvement with the education of other Christian women. I am now a therapist and specialize in working with abused children. In addition, I serve on the board of directors of a child care center and a battered women's shelter.

At the time of my ordeal and decision, I was strongly opposed to abortion. It took me several years to work out in my own life and in my faith this contradiction between what I believed and the choice I had made. I now appreciate how critical it is for each person, as an image-bearer of God, to make sure that she never allows anyone to intervene in her own personal relationship with God.

We can never know what God is doing in another person's life.

10

Trying Freedom, Finding Myself §

Bonnie Moser

I grew up in a loving, committed, Christian, socially conservative family in a small farming community in southeastern Colorado. Our church and its teachings played a major role in my formation with mostly positive and lasting results. But like many whose adolescence is governed fairly strictly, I struggled as I became independent. I had many questions and experimented with a lifestyle I had always been warned against. As a result, my Christian faith now is defined a bit differently from my parents, but it is a solid faith nonetheless.

My first years away from home, in the early 1970s, were spent at small denominational colleges in Kansas and Indiana. After my junior year, I decided to take a break to figure out what I really wanted to do. From a perspective 15 years later, that decision seems valid, but at the time this choice made me feel like a failure—someone apparently unstable and unready for adulthood. After a summer of traveling with friends around the western United States, I moved with a friend to Pennsylvania, where I managed to land a secretarial job at a church-related relief and development agency.

This was my first year to be both away from home and away from a conservative college dormitory setting. Soon I began living two lives. At work I was responsible and upstanding, but at home with my roommates it was party time. We were on our own, doing all the things we had been taught were wrong. I enjoyed the freedom, but at the same time felt irresponsible and dishonest. I wasn't particularly convicted about the sinfulness of my actions, but I was uncomfortable with not being able to mesh my two lives. Because of self-deprecation and my lack of self-confidence, I vacillated; it took me a while to get up the initiative to rectify the situation.

Getting pregnant was the final jolt I needed to sit up and begin making changes. The father was not much more than a passing acquaintance for whom I felt little affection. I was distressed when the pregnancy test came back positive, but I rather coldly assessed the situation and concluded that abortion was the only alternative. I don't think I once considered going through with the pregnancy. I also didn't think about any of the moral dilemmas. No other alternative seriously entered my mind.

With my roommates' help, I furtively made an appointment in a state abortion clinic. Before the pregnancy was into the sixth week, I had an abortion by suction. The procedure itself was painless and since it took place on a Saturday morning, I was able to have it done without missing work. Of course, no one there knew anything about my situation.

Emotionally I felt rather removed from the abortion. To me it simply marked the end of a sloppy and irresponsible way of living. I was frustrated and angry with myself for allowing it to happen, but I didn't feel ruined or debased. It was not a good situation, but it was something that had to be done.

That would have been that, as far as I was emotionally concerned, had it not been for a breach of confidence within the Planned Parenthood system. I was 21 years old and financially independent from my parents, but apparently someone at Planned Parenthood, where I had gone for my pregnancy test and received a referral to the abortion clinic, felt it was his or her duty to make an anonymous phone call to my parents to inform them of the situation. (Unfortunately, I was too young and insecure to make this betrayal of confidence known to Planned Parenthood and to voice my shock at such a breach of trust.)

Of course, my parents responded with hurt and confusion, though they remained supportive of me as their daughter. They called me the night before the abortion was to be performed. Although their knowing did not change my feelings about having the abortion, it did add anxiety to the situation. That phone call told me that instead of just messing up my own life, I had also hurt them badly. But at that point I had already made my personal decision to clean up my lifestyle; I didn't need to be convinced to do that.

To this day I feel that my parents could have been spared that pain, but perhaps the one benefit was that it helped them face the fact that unwanted pregnancies and abortions do occur, even in their immediate world. They did show incredible tolerance and openness toward me, difficult as it was for them to understand. Perhaps going through this experience with me helped to prepare for other difficult situations that my sisters have challenged them with over the years. I have been blessed with a truly loving family.

With the abortion behind me, I made serious changes in my lifestyle that left me feeling more in control. Gradually I regained my self-confidence and began to be more involved in the community and in a house church, which was part of a larger church-building effort. At work I moved into a more challenging and responsible position, which I very much enjoyed. It was a very positive and happy time for me.

In the next several years I learned and travelled and had many formative experiences as a single, childless person. After three years with the development agency, I was offered a position in Kinshasa, Zaire, Africa. Although it was difficult to leave a community where I was very happy, I was intrigued by the challenge and looked forward to studying French in Europe as preparation. I lived in Brussels for six months, learned some French, and managed to see a bit of Europe.

Zaire was an entirely different experience. For over two years I was the support person for 30 volunteers working in different parts of the country. I learned a lot and made some wonderful and lasting friends—my husband among them. I had a (mostly) wonderful time as I observed and absorbed a totally different culture and economic and political system.

None of this would have been possible had I been a single parent. This exposure to life in developing countries changed my view of the world and my place in it. I can better understand what most people in the world are up against. I feel compelled to make more responsible lifestyle decisions and share my experiences with family and friends. At a deeper level, living outside my own culture, single and on my own, greatly contributed to my self-confidence and sense of direction.

In 1980 I returned to the United States and enrolled in a college-degree program in small business management. My husband and I were married after he had completed law school. He accepted a job in international law, which eventually brought us to Brussels, Belgium. Our first daughter was born there in 1984, followed by another in 1987. As a family we are now very involved in a small church group and in various ecumenical activities in Belgium and beyond.

When I reflect on my abortion decision so many years ago, I see that things have worked out very well—and not just for me personally. Because I was free to learn and work without having to support a child, I have been able to become a person who has much more to give to society, as well as to the children that I now have. Then I was neither emotionally nor financially ready to care for a child; now I am.

Of course, having experienced childbearing now, I think back to that pregnancy and the child-that-might-have-been with different emotions. I can't wish that I had handled it differently, but I do recognize the self-preserving aspects of my decision. I had behaved irresponsibly and perhaps I should have paid a greater price. But what interests me more than judging myself is trying to understand why I was so sexually and physically irresponsible. I was an intelligent, educated person and I knew the risks. Nevertheless, I was in denial. To have taken precautions would have meant admitting to my rather frivolous sexual activity. I thought I was being sophisticated and free, but I was actually playing mind games with myself.

From that experience I conclude that one of the best things we can do for our children is to talk with them about sex and sexuality in ways that don't involve all the guilt and denial. Somehow they need to learn to respect themselves and be responsible physically, even if they choose to be occasionally irresponsible in their relationships. Perhaps if they really do learn self-respect, they may be able to do without irresponsible relationships.

Regarding the abortion issue, I am very much pro-choice. How can a few predominantly male legislators or Supreme Court justices decide what rules apply to something so personal and potentially life-changing as an unwanted pregnancy? Nevertheless, abortion should not be seen as another form of birth control. There *are* moral considerations regarding abortion, difficult as they may be to define in a unilateral way. If we are going to decrease the number of abortions, we need to present better alternatives to women with unwanted pregnancies. Financial as well as emotional support may need to be provided over a fairly lengthy period of time. Consideration of the overwhelming and continuing responsibility of raising a child needs to be a part of every discussion of abortion. This job is something to be neither taken lightly nor easily tossed aside to adoptive parents.

There is no easy answer, but a good starting place is to talk openly with our children and to teach them more responsible attitudes toward themselves and their sexuality.

11

Hepatitis, Anorexia — and Pregnancy? §

Terri Myers

W hen I had my abortion, I wasn't much more than a kid myself. True, I was 21 years old, but I wasn't as mature as my years implied. Even though I had matured sexually rather early, the other levels of maturity were not in sync. From the perspective of emotional maturity and practical sense, I was a good many years behind my appearance. As the popular slogan used to go, "God wasn't finished with me yet." Of course, at that time I didn't realize God was doing anything with me anyway. Atheism was in the air in the 1960s and I was hungry to be a part of the vast, exciting world outside my ethnically-mixed, working-class Catholic neighborhood in Philadelphia. I made some mistakes.

My first mistake was in rejecting the church of my youth—the Roman Catholic church—because from my teenaged perspective it seemed corrupt and full of hypocrites who pledged to love but were not loving. Since youth expects perfection, I threw the baby out with the bath water as I dissociated myself from my church and my faith. This choice left me in a spiritual void— which I began to fill with romantic love and sex, at least temporarily.

There were many large, extended families in our rough-and-tumble neighborhood, and there were always a sizable number of teenage girls getting pregnant out of wedlock. Usually a shotgun wedding was arranged, but poverty, alcoholism and domestic violence were not so easily put right. The cycle tended to perpetuate itself. While I was growing up, I saw the misery of some of those pregnant girls—15- or 16-years old, staying in the house and missing out on life because they thought themselves unsightly while pregnant, or because there was some trouble in arranging a marriage for them, or because they were the victims of ongoing sexual abuse.

I never dreamed I would someday be in a similar plight. I had always been at the top of my class and thought of myself as destined for college or for a career, not for motherhood. In fact, I questioned whether romance would ever enter my life since I was such a lonely bookworm as a child and young teenager. Things changed, however, not just for me, but for many of our institutions during the 1960s.

During high school my resistance to sexual involvement was partially overcome by the sexual liberation becoming prevalent at that time—and I wanted to be contemporary in every way at that stage in my life. I was also swept along by nature, by my tremendous need to feel loved, and by the comfort of being hugged and kissed by my boyfriend. These forces, along with my own passivity and curiosity about this unfolding experience, all combined to push back my barriers a little at a time. My first two relationships with a boy lasted a long time—a total of three years—but were incomplete sexually, so there was very little danger of pregnancy. My mother did not try to scare me about pregnancy—she didn't have to. I was plenty scared of that possibility.

My second major mistake came when I was 19 and got involved with friends who were using drugs. Eventually I tried them myself, partly because my other options for growth had been cut off. My neighborhood was sinking socio-economically. I had let my grades slip during high school and had lost out on any scholarship opportunities, so I was struggling to work and put myself through college, living at times in apartments with friends or at home.

I had always been introverted, bookish, and not too street-wise. Furthermore, my parents and I were not communicating. They assumed I knew things about life that I didn't know, and there was a big age difference between us; they were involved with their own health problems and financial setbacks.

To complicate matters, I was passionate about my choices and beliefs. I always took extreme positions. At my first job, working for a credit union, I realized that the owners were bilking the poor—and I quit. If I thought I was right, I would not compromise. I thought drugs expanded the mind—everyone was saying that then—and I wanted to grow in that area. For introverts especially, drugs are a subtle temptation. Taking them did not seem unethical to me. Naïvely I didn't think drugs could hurt people, and they ended up hurting me.

I was first introduced to drugs by an attractive man who used drugs but did not demand sex. In fact, he seemed totally uninterested in sex. I felt safe with him and lived with him for a year. I saw myself as an observer of life, but I decided I needed to *experience* life as well and so began to use marijuana and then

LSD. My third major mistake came when I dabbled in heroin and digoxin injections. This was the low point of my life. From this point on, my life improved, except for a few short dips at the beginning of the upward trail.

My experiences among the drug-addicts allowed me to observe what real degradation, disease and desperation are—and yet how even in a hellish world, there could be caring, kindness and even occasional generosity. Nevertheless, I soon saw how limited generosity and other virtues were with these people. Locked in a desperate selfishness and duplicity around the need for a drug, a part of each person wanted to seek good, but they were trapped in sin against their own will.

In the midst of all this, I contracted Hepatitis B and spent my 20th year at home recovering from that. I was also diagnosed by the doctor as having malnutrition. Today they would probably have called it anorexia, but I got off drugs and considered myself lucky not to have become truly addicted.

As soon as I was marginally well, I struck out into life and moved to Massachusetts where I became involved with a group interested in Eastern spiritual practices—yoga and meditation—along with a vegetarian diet. I was still weak and underweight, not fully recovered, so I hoped a life focused on health and spirituality would be beneficial. In this clean-living environment I regained my morale and some sense of vision and self-esteem.

At this point I became interested in finding God again. I wanted to grow as a person and this setting offered me the opportunity. I might have even regained my health if it hadn't been for the strictly vegetarian diet. It was probably good for me in many ways, except that liver disease requires high protein for recovery, and our protein intake was questionable.

In this yoga community we considered ourselves very liberated and didn't believe in the necessity of marriage. Nevertheless I slept with only one man during the nine months I was there. Our relationship must have been difficult for Bruce because nearly every night I cried before going to sleep, and I was weak and sickly. He had to put up with a fair amount of criticism about me from other members of the group. Bruce was patient with me, but finally a time came when he felt he'd had enough. We stopped sleeping together and only rarely did so during the last few months that we both lived in the community.

On the last night we ever slept together, however, I became pregnant. I knew it had happened because something inside me cried out "NO!" at the moment of ejaculation. I was very upset. I had been using the same method of birth control throughout our relationship—a diaphragm with spermicide during my fertile days—but my method of calculating them was somewhat imprecise, based upon the cycles of the moon more than upon physiological signs. Though there had been no conception in all those months of frequent intercourse, that night I knew that what I least wanted had in fact happened. I knew I wanted to love a baby who would come into my life, but only when I could provide a loving family and home. To have a baby when these things were not possible was not a part of my dream.

During the three weeks I had to wait to take the pregnancy test, I did some soul-searching and knew I did not want to bring a child into the world without a father. I did not even feel I *could*. I was terribly afraid, but I couldn't admit that fear to myself. I was open to keeping the baby if the father would make a commitment to us and support me in that process, or even if the group would do so. But of course Bruce didn't, and they didn't, and I couldn't do it alone. I felt the full responsibility should not fall on me alone. I was angry as well as afraid.

I could hardly take care of myself, let alone a baby. My health was so poor that I couldn't sustain a full day's work; I needed to sleep and at times the need would simply overpower me. Though my mother had always told me I could come home if I ever got pregnant (not in those exact words, but we both knew what she meant), I couldn't face returning to that place of no growth—my old neighborhood of drugs and sickness and decay. I wanted to live. I was very upset with those in the community who accused me of trying to hold on to Bruce through this pregnancy, and I wanted to prove them wrong.

As I waited and tried to make a decision, I engaged in theological sophistries. I concluded that God knew I wasn't going to have the baby and therefore would not be so foolish as to put a real soul into the microscopic body within me. At least I hoped that might be true. I must have numbed myself to any other possibility because somehow I went through the whole process of finding out that I was pregnant and obtaining the abortion as if I were sleep-walking. I had the abortion at the earliest opportunity, after only three weeks of pregnancy. Many pregnancies are sloughed off naturally during that time. I preferred to think of it that way.

Most of the people around me—all strangers—seemed overtly or covertly to disapprove of me. No one offered me the hand of love. Since then I have found supportive friends, and they have wondered if I could have carried the baby to term anyway at that time in my life, but we'll never know for sure. The baby might have been severely damaged. Between the hepatitis and the anorexia, I was as skinny as a rail.

During that time I reviewed the last three years. It seemed they had been a spiral descent into the mystery of darkness. I saw how evil can begin with small sins and end with death. I remembered a passage in the Bible describing this process: "For God ... tempts no one; but each person is tempted ... by his own desire. Then desire when it has conceived gives birth to sin; and sin when it is full-grown brings forth death" (Jas 1:13-15). The people I knew who were using drugs were sliding down into death, and I myself had participated in a death, one that seemed as if it ought to be easy because it was so small and hidden. But this small death had a tremendous impact on me. It was the nadir of my personal journey through the valley of the shadow of death. There was nowhere for me to go but into God's light.

After the abortion I was still confused and very vulnerable. I moved from Massachusetts to California to live with an old friend who had the courage to bring her child into the world without a father, as many more of my women friends and acquaintances were choosing to do. She had also come out as a lesbian.

Shortly after getting to California, I moved into a small apartment of my own, but I had few friends and soon realized that the world was a pretty hard place after all. I knew that I never wanted another abortion to happen in my life, and after two more brief and confused relationships, I finally realized that my life was headed in a destructive direction, not at all toward my hopes and dreams. I recognized how frightened and unloved I felt and began to miss my parents, a genteel elderly couple. I realized that whatever my problems had been at home, life there was better than what I had here. A prodigal daughter, admitting defeat, I decided to go home at age 22 to start a new chapter in my life.

I returned to my parents' home and, more importantly, to their values. This time my life changed in earnest. Finally I had the courage and determination to live successfully in the surroundings where my parents lived. Our neighborhood had gone from bad to worse in the years I had been gone. It was now little better than a slum, and considerable drug use was going on in the area. I found that I had great reserves of will power and independence after all as I faced that culture.

Though I participated in some neighborhood activities, I kept away from drugs. Achieving this was a tremendous growth in discipline for me. I stopped expecting the world to satisfy my needs or make my life exciting. I was lonely a great deal, but I began to look inside myself for direction and meaning in life instead of trying to find it in my peers. I began to read again, to enjoy my own company and to develop a mind of my own.

As I learned to spend my evenings reading again, I recovered my old introverted style, keeping a journal and learning about myself. I even stopped smoking marijuana—which had been a powerful psychological addiction for me—and began to read sacred scripture again—the Bible and the Koran. These books supported me in my resolve to change my life.

I especially loved the Book of Proverbs and the moral and theological musings of the Koran. I found the latter rather harsh about sin, but no harsher than life itself in the consequences of sin. I began to find myself praying again, simply feeling the presence of God. And eventually, one cold and snow-bound winter night, I had a very powerful experience of Christ's healing light. The assurance came that I was loved by God and forgiven for my past wrongs and failures.

As I began to pray, read the Bible and listen for the prompting of the Holy Spirit in my life, I began to experience many healings, especially on the emotional level. My mother had become a Catholic charismatic, and I occasionally accompanied her to prayer meetings. I began reading C.S. Lewis and was challenged by his writings. My life became established on a new foundation—one of prayer, service to others and a sense of commitment and responsibility toward God.

I realized that I had to be responsible about my own sexuality; I knew I never wanted to repeat what I had gone through. I wanted to be in a relationship with a man who could be responsible and committed to me and any children we might conceive. Soon after coming to this resolution, I met my husband, Bill. My health began to improve. I still had dark times ahead, but through them I came to know Christ.

After we married, Bill and I moved to another city where I joined a prayer group and did my best to be supportive of other group members who were in need. For some reason we attracted a fair number of disabled or mentally disturbed people—some who had been victimized by the social upheaval of the 1960s and 70s, others who were in transition or living difficult lives—beautiful people but some more difficult to love than others. Before long I was part of the leadership team of the group and did my best to organize the meetings, plan extra events and lead teaching and sharing sessions.

Nevertheless, there were still unresolved issues in my life, primarily vocational. I desired to be a homemaker and mother, but I never conceived another child. Many of my friends and acquaintances who had abortions later experienced the healing of bearing other children, but this particular healing was never to be mine. This emptiness in my home caused me to have tragic feelings. Besides the grief and suffering I underwent, I also felt simply frustrated and unfulfilled vocationally. I wanted to work at something I believed in.

Friends urged me to study for the ministry, and after I did that, I began to study traditional Chinese medicine. At the present time I don't know what form my religious ministry will take, but I still feel an inner sense of devotion to service. I trust these two fields of study will enable me to be of use to others.

My life was really changed by my abortion. Perhaps completing the pregnancy would have changed my life in equally serious ways, but it wasn't the choice I made at that time. I do know that my abortion was part of a struggle back toward health and a good direction for my life. I regret the period of drugs and self-destructiveness that led to the abortion, but I do know that God has forgiven me.

Looking back, I am convinced that abortion must remain available as an option. A woman's child-bearing capacity is intimately part of her identity. Even when we choose celibacy or contraception, we are never unaware of the potential of creating life. An unwanted pregnancy can strike the core of our sense of well-being, as can the threat of infertility and childlessness. Issues related to our children, or lack of children, cause us untold suffering and can direct the entire shape and tenor of our lives. Therefore, decisions about how a woman handles her potential of motherhood cannot rest with an impersonal governmental body, either judicial or legislative. These are personal matters and must be decided on a personal basis. Each woman must make her own decision.

Along with choice, however, to prevent the overuse of abortion, if I had come to early adulthood with a clearer knowledge of my own body, of conception and contraception, of the impact of drugs and the dangers of hepatitis and anorexia, my life would have been very different. Let us give that knowledge, along with a sense of God's presence and support, to our young people today.

12

Our Pain Becomes
Our Power §

Lucine Gadoorian

Three years ago through the crisis of an unplanned pregnancy, I began to understand the power of pain as a teacher and even a healer. Pain can be a rite of passage to wisdom. We cannot avoid the presence of pain, but we do have the power to change how we approach and process pain, gaining a deeper understanding of our motives, needs and actions. My experience with abortion opened me to communication with the wise woman within me; I began to accept pain and its transformative power. That experience began the process of coming home to myself, a journey I continue today.

Choosing abortion was a complex and difficult process, but for me it was ultimately the more compassionate choice. The anti-abortion movement portrays a woman who chooses to have an abortion as evil, sacrificing her baby out of selfish motives. But this myth simply doesn't fit my experience and I doubt that it fits the experience of many other women. In my case, we decided together—this being, myself and my partner—that we could not lovingly become a family now—not with the commitment, patience and grounding that is essential to healthy parenting. Considering the whole picture, we did not use abortion as "the easy way out." We did not evade responsibility in choosing to terminate our pregnancy; on the contrary, we decided that abortion was the more responsible thing to do.

As an American Armenian from a Christian background, I was raised in the Episcopal church and peripherally in the Armenian Apostolic (Orthodox) church. Until a few years ago I identified simply as a Christian. Now, without denying that Christian background, I continue to explore what religion, spiritual practice and community mean to me outside of any institutional religious group. I find it more fulfilling to ask questions and celebrate ritual without the confines of an organization.

Zachariah and I fell in love with each other three years ago. We met working at a coöperative in Vermont while both of us were searching for spiritual equilibrium, trying to unfold and incorporate spiritual practice in our daily lives. I had been out of college for two years and had undertaken a variety of exhilarating tasks, including teaching in the Middle East for a year. Newly committed to going inside, to working with the process of coming home to myself, I had left my familiar life in New York City and moved to rural Vermont.

When we met, Zach was about to depart for California where he planned to spend the summer at a monastery. After he left, we began to miss each other intensely. Zach finally returned to Vermont earlier than planned so we could be together.

Life was blissful for us in the beginning—a fairy tale romance. Each of us had high and somewhat unrealistic ideals for this relationship. We had even chosen to share a home. As with many new couples, sex was an important part of our life to-gether. We decided not to use chemical birth control, but rather to avoid intercourse during the fertile part of my cycle.

Soon, though, the fairy tale began to go awry; the "happily ever after" changed to serious mutual disillusionment. In the euphoria of togetherness, Zach and I had neglected our own personal growth processes. The relationship became a crutch to shadow our insecurities and to avoid dealing with our own feelings. Within two months of his return, we were exasperated with each other and with our own selves, neither of us sure what we truly wanted to give or reap from this relationship.

In the mire of this disillusionment, my usually punctual period didn't happen. "Must be stress," I thought. "My peri-od's waiting for the full moon." The full moon waxed, then began to wane—still no blood. Next I began to notice that the smells of certain foods were making me sick. "But I can't be pregnant," I thought. "I felt myself ovulate. I must be having menstrual cramps." Two weeks of waiting were enough to waken my suspicion, however. I knew somehow that I was indeed pregnant. So it was: my pregnancy test at Planned Parent-hood came out positive.

Immediately I knew that I was unprepared to make the in-tensely loving commitment to raise a child. From deep within my being I knew that I could not have this baby. Agonizing as it was to carry out, the decision to terminate my pregnancy was sound—as were the motives behind it. In the years since the abortion, I have not regretted that decision. I have been thankful for having the opportunity to do it safely and legally. Time has also reaffirmed what I knew immediately upon becoming aware of my pregnancy—that I was not ready to be a mother.

Since my teen years I had told myself that if I were to become pregnant before I was ready to raise a child, I would have to end the pregnancy. Nonetheless, when this crisis came, I needed to question my prefabricated decision and consider the full range of options. Bearing the baby only to put her up for adoption was out of the question; this world is already over-populated with humans and there are millions of parent-less children. I refused to satisfy some couple waiting for a light-skinned baby, as I would not want to subject any child to the implied racism in such a preference. Moreover, I knew that if I were to carry her for nine months, I would feel too closely connected with the baby to give her away.

I also knew that raising a child myself was an impossibility at this time in my life. I had just reached a time of personal stability, beginning to know myself and understand life. Were I to have a baby, my situation and that of my child would become infinitely more vulnerable—emotionally and financially. It was not the environment in which I would want to welcome a child into this world, though another woman in a similar position might have made another decision.

I considered other possibilities with Zach, with this Being (as we called the life beginning within me) and with other friends, but instinctively I knew I must terminate the pregnancy. Unfortunately, I intellectualized the decision process and numbed myself emotionally and spiritually to the reality of my pregnancy—until the abortion was just a few hours away.

Logical, reasoned, resolved, I distanced myself from this experience. I feared I might change my mind and decide to have a baby I was not ready to raise. Above all, I did not want to remain in a state of indecision; I wanted to make a choice and act.

What I really needed was spiritual counseling to help me feel the full presence of my pregnancy—not to change my decision to abort, but to understand it better and be at peace with it. I needed to be in touch with what was happening to me in body and spirit as well as in my head. Zach and I were both desperate for such guidance.

As helpful as it was to talk with women friends, especially those who had experienced abortion, it was not enough. We also went to a reproductive health clinic for counseling. These clinics are great for advising people in practical matters concerning reproduction and abortion—but not for the spiritual needs.

The woman with whom we met was understanding yet reserved and empirical. She reassured us that most women felt great relief after an abortion—that was all. Her approach seemed rather simplistic; I knew my emotions would be much more complex than that, and they were, though relief was certainly part of it.

In spite of confusion and denial, I was able to admit that I liked the feeling of being pregnant. Instinctively, I was gentle with my body—eating well and giving myself lots of rest. It felt good to be in this special situation. The bond, the intimate connection with this Being within and around me, both physically and spiritually, was intense. I had felt her with me—a strong feminine presence—even before I was physically pregnant. It seemed we were meant to be together at this time.

After that first appointment, I confirmed my decision and began the search for a clinic in which to do it. I was adamant that a woman perform the abortion, for the procedure itself is so invasive. I finally found a feminist, woman-operated clinic (since then it has been the target of violent anti-abortion protests and raids). At this clinic, male partners are allowed to be present during the abortion, and I wanted Zach with me. We were both in this together and equally responsible.

The day of the abortion Zach and I rose early to prepare ourselves with cleansing and prayer. Both of us meditated silently, first alone, then together. I talked to the Being growing inside me and asked for her forgiveness, trying to communicate to her that I was doing this out of love.

We arrived at the clinic in mid-morning and immediately met with a counselor. She thoroughly explained the procedure, promising to be with us during the abortion to talk us through it. She was sympathetic to our situation, but again, out of necessity, her approach remained somewhat impersonal. Her job was to provide information and medical assistance, not the spiritual support I desperately needed.

We set an appointment to have the abortion a few hours later and left the clinic. It was then that I lost control. Realizing my imminent course of action, I panicked, saying, "I can't do this, not yet."

Zach gently reminded me that I didn't have to do it that day. I desperately wanted to believe him, but something inside of me would not let go. We sat in my car for almost an hour.

Wanting to celebrate this Being's life and to validate her presence, I felt moved to name her. I gave her a first name, Anahid (an ancient Armenian name meaning "mother goddess") and Zach gave her a second, Morningstar. Both names were to reflect the powerful duality of her spirit—ancient wisdom and new freshness—what her strong feminine presence had communicated to me.

When I had calmed down a bit, we decided to gain some distance from the experience by walking around the town; we weren't due back at the clinic for a few hours. Walking worked to soothe me superficially, but I felt an undertone of doom the whole time, knowing that the events of this day were not simply business as usual and could not be reduced to that.

What I really needed was to wait instead of insisting on acting right away. It was early in my pregnancy (five to six weeks) so I could have waited, but I did not want to prolong my agony, that of the Being and that of Zach. Consequently, I felt deprived; I wanted to continue in this state of harmonious communion with this Being in my womb, but I felt that doing so was an unattainable luxury, that I couldn't actually let myself *be* pregnant. Somewhat numbed to the reality of this pregnancy, I acted too soon.

When we returned to my car, I again became hysterical, feeling that I had no clarity or perspective on my situation. Yet again I questioned my decision, asking myself: "Am I forgetting her and thinking only of myself? Maybe I am ready to have a baby and be a conscious, committed mother. Maybe I've been deluding myself."

Though a part of me wanted to have this child, I knew I had to get my act together before I could do any conscious mothering. I felt consumed and alone, torn by my polarized feelings yet adamant about not remaining in a state of indecision.

Back at the clinic, I felt strangled by my anxiety. A quickening sense of urgency immobilized me. I insisted on speaking with a counselor again, hoping she could help pull me out of this vortex of confusion. Now I realize that I was desperately searching outside myself for perspective, when what I needed was time in which to come to it on my own—but I also needed spiritual guidance to do this.

The second counselor was young and, though she tried, not too helpful. Sensing my frustration, she brought in the woman who was to perform my abortion. My desperation was growing as I searched for something these women could not give me—a spiritual point of view. I scraped what I could from them and interpreted it in my own terms, yet still felt empty and isolated.

Throughout the day, everyone with whom I spoke at the clinic asked me, "Are you sure this is what you want to do?"

Though I appreciated their concern, I could only reply that it wasn't a question of *wanting* to have an abortion or not; I didn't *want* to have an abortion. I had chosen to terminate my pregnancy rather than continue it. How could one *want* to endure the agonizing experience of terminating a pregnancy?

This older woman, compassionate, patient and experienced, was more helpful. She counseled me to wait a day or two and then said, "Envision what it will be like for you if you wake up tomorrow, the next day, two weeks from now if you are pregnant—and if you are not pregnant."

A strong answer welled up within me and I whispered, "I can't be pregnant any more." Feeling compelled to go through with it, I assured her and Zach, "Yes, I'm sure."

There was truth in that statement: I was sure that I couldn't go through with this pregnancy. But I was also sure that I was not ready to have the abortion; I said yes because it seemed more compassionate not to put this Being through prolonged agony. Somehow I could not give myself the option to abort later. I needed to wait, but I did not want to return to indecision.

I asked the Being to leave my body and at first felt strong resistance—which was most distressing. I felt torn and as if there was no time for delay; I really wanted her to stay with me but felt compelled to ask her to leave. I heard a voice screaming inside, "What about ME!"

Maybe it was myself, maybe it was this being. I don't know. But then suddenly I felt bathed by a sense of peace from her. I believed that she was safely outside of my body and would be in no pain from the abortion. Just as I had moved to protect her, she was now protecting me. I thought, "Please forgive me, Anahid Morningstar. I love you—I believe I'm doing this out of love."

We went upstairs to the room where the abortion was to be done. I was scared but determined not to give in. The woman performing the abortion was kind and gentle, making the experience easier than it could have been. It was also a great comfort to have Zach present with me. We practiced slow deep breathing together and he held my hand. At one point the physical pain became so intense I bit Zach's hand.

As soon as it was over, I began to shake uncontrollably. Exhausted and overwhelmed from the shock of the experience, I just wanted to go home and sleep.

Soon after terminating my pregnancy, I felt newly grounded and powerful. At the same time, my relationship with Zach developed an unprecedented tension. Although I was clear about my own focus and goals, our relationship increasingly lacked communication. I had gained more of a sense of place in the world and knew I didn't want distractions. I wanted to be, to live alone.

Nevertheless, I still felt unsettled and unfinished about my abortion, as if it were not yet complete. I needed closure on this experience to make peace with this being we had named Anahid Morningstar and to remember and celebrate her. At first I thought of doing something like planting a tree in her name, but soon I realized that I wanted to have a memorial service for her.

It would be the most healing action for all of us.

Zach knew of a woman Episcopal priest with whom he had met for counseling a few years before; we wrote to her, explaining our feelings about this abortion and how unsettled, disheartened and in need of guidance we both were. She responded immediately, acknowledging the loss and lack of direction I was feeling. She also affirmed my choice as an act of compassion and offered to perform a memorial service with us, adding that "sincerely performing rites of passage for her would be healing not only to her but to you as well."

It was refreshing to be reminded that I too deserved healing. To have someone acknowledge and validate my pain was a great comfort. We arranged a date for the service and meanwhile I made a picture and a poem about Anahid Morningstar.

On the day of the memorial service, Zach and I had a long discussion with the priest. She then reviewed with us the format of the service and we chose some invocations. I felt content that I was doing the right thing, but I also felt compelled to resolve everything with this memorial service, that it had to represent the final letting go. Again the complexity of my feelings reflected the complexity of life.

In a sacred space, Zach and I first offer fruit to the altar—beautiful, colorful, bright fruit. We light incense and sit in silent meditation. Zach and I name the Being, calling her by her names Anahid and Morningstar. She is here with us. Praying and chanting in unison, in community we acknowledge this time and space—its sacredness, its vulnerability, its intensity. The steady beat of Zach's drum matches the rhythm of our words. We read a poem called "Flowers" for Anahid Morningstar. Music, prayer, poetry, incense, silence, tears, fruit. All senses. All experiences of life in this space. Birth death death birth and all that is in between in this ever-spiraling cycle of generations.

Remembering Anahid Morningstar with love, sending her my love, asking her forgiveness, feeling her love and my love for her. Feelings of sadness from both her and me. A dancing-yet-still liberation. As the service ends, I ask God to be with her, my tears again flowing. I become the tears and let myself be held by those around me.

After the memorial service, I realized that this rite of passage could not resolve everything. Though I had expected it to complete the healing, it was only another step in the process that began immediately after the abortion. To make more progress I decided to work with a therapist, and doing so has helped me acknowledge my anger, become aware of my feelings, and become more honest and more gentle with myself. I am still confident that both the abortion and the commemorative service were the right choice for me.

Zach and I spent another year working to transform our relationship; after much struggle, we parted. Soon I left Vermont to study feminist theology. I now work at a shelter for battered women and have begun training as a midwife.

Though the process of choosing and enduring an abortion was agonizing, I remain strongly pro-choice. Being pro-choice does not mean insisting that every unplanned or unwanted pregnancy be terminated. Rather it means that every woman faced with a pregnancy should have the right to choose the option that's best for her: to continue with her pregnancy or to safely, legally and affordably terminate it. We must trust that our *own* choice is the right thing to do, and we must have the opportunity to carry out that choice.

Pregnancy is too highly personal, spiritual and complex a matter for any law to govern. Reproductive laws incorrectly assume that women are a monolith with uniform experience and access to resources. The mere idea of such legislation is deeply misogynist. On the contrary, we are individuals, discrete and sacred yet connected through the powerful web of womankind.

Today I fear for the future of our choice, so vulnerable in the hands of the religious/political powers. As I write, three states and one U.S. territory have re-criminalized abortion. Poor women of all racial and ethnic groups are increasingly at risk, particularly women of color who have been denied access to resources by the white heterosexual patriarchy. I shudder, remembering a film about a woman in France who was sentenced to death for performing abortions during World War II. This nightmare of the past is looming on our own horizons.

As we face the threat of losing legal rights over our own bodies, women are taking reproductive power into our own hands. In my future work as a midwife, I hope to be a part of that.

13

Of Toddlers, Twins and
A Tubal Ligation §

Angela Alvarez

I was probably a DES baby. After my mother had my older brother in 1947, she had a number of miscarriages and stillbirths for the next 13 years. The doctors prescribed various drugs—including diethylstilbestrol, a synthetic estrogen—to enable her to complete a pregnancy. Finally I was born in 1960. During the '70s the press began reporting problems of daughters born to women who had taken DES, and these problems fit my experience: late menstruation with a wide variety of gynecological problems starting at menses. The doctors told me that since DES seemed to have affected me, there was a strong possibility I would continue to have gynecological problems and probably have a hysterectomy before I got too far into my thirties. The message was: if you are going to have children, have them while you are young.

As things turned out, I got married when I was 18—and was divorced before I was 19 and before my son Gabriel was born.

From the beginning I have been a single parent. Two years later I got pregnant again with twins, Jessica and Daniel. Although I had been involved with their father and wanted to have a baby with him, at first I hadn't been able to conceive. I had prayed for a baby, but after a while the relationship began breaking up. The last night that I was with him, I got pregnant with *two* babies—a boy and a girl. I felt as if God had answered my prayer because I really wanted to have kids; if we had stayed together I'd probably have a dozen kids now.

My parents, who have been married 40 years, were cradle Catholics who became Protestant Christians as adults. They sent me to Catholic schools in Los Angeles for a number of years, but we were members of a series of Protestant churches—Lutheran, then later Methodist, and others. Because most of our extended family are still Catholic, we always participated in all the Catholic holidays and weddings—more as a cultural habit than a religious practice. We also read the Bible a lot, and I was expected to memorize chapter and verse.

My mother had been adopted when she was young and came to the U.S. from Puerto Rico just before World War II. Years later she located her natural sister—who turned out to be mean and hateful toward her—resenting that my mother had been adopted by a prosperous family who sent her to private schools. My mother felt bereft of family and when I was born she was 36 and wanted someone who could be a daughter/sister/friend to her. When I got into my teenage years and didn't want to be her friend anymore, she was really hurt and we went through a period of estrangement during my teens and early twenties.

After my strict upbringing, I was ready to strike out on my own at age 17. Even though I loved my parents—and still do— sometimes their craziness was just too much. Besides my problematic relationship with my mother, my father had become an alcoholic (he's now sober) and my mother was totally preoccupied with my father's drinking. At any rate, I was packed and gone two weeks after I graduated from high school. As soon as I left home, I began going to Catholic church and soon became a Catholic. In fact, when I got pregnant with Gabriel, my parents didn't even know I was married. They had met my husband when we were dating, but after I left home I didn't feel that my life was their business.

Gabriel was three when I had the twins, and by then my parents were involved with us again and glad to be grandparents. Soon I went back to work—and back on the pill. I was also attending college to finish my bachelor's degree. With the kids in day care plus my job, life was a whirlwind. A friend of mine from the Mothers of Twins Club called the first year "Double Diaper Derby". You don't remember anything because all you're doing is changing and feeding them. Looking back on that time, I'm really glad I had children when I was young because I *know* I would not have had the energy to do it now.

I was dating and on the pill but somehow when the twins were just a year old, I got pregnant again—with a man who definitely was not marriage material. I knew I had reached my limit and could not handle a four-year old, the twins and a new baby alone. I thought about putting the baby up for adoption, but it didn't seem right. The situation was clear: my birth control had failed and I had a choice to make.

I was raised pro-choice. My mother lost her best friend in the '40s to a back-alley abortionist in Los Angeles—an experience that had profoundly affected my mother. After that she worked for three years at General Hospital during World War II. I grew up on her stories of women she saw come in with botched abortions and attempted self-abortions. These experiences convinced her that abortion should be an alternative for women.

Even before I found out I was pregnant a third time, I had broken up with the father, and at that point he started becoming violent with me. He even threatened that he was going to beat me until I lost this baby. Soon after that, when I was about seven weeks along, I had an abortion. I was sad but I felt God would forgive me—and that God knew that I had to do what I had to do. Certainly having an abortion would be better than having another baby and not being able to raise it properly.

After the abortion I really needed support from someone or perhaps from a group, but I could find no one. I didn't tell my parents, who by then were involved in a fundamentalist church. I was back in the Catholic church attending adult education classes, but I didn't expect any understanding there. Besides, as a single parent with three kids, working and in school, I didn't have time to agonize and grieve or process my feelings the way I probably would have if my circumstances had been different. Basically the situation was, "I have to survive, I have to keep going, I have to get through this abortion somehow."

Going to the clinic to arrange the abortion, I had requested a tubal ligation and signed the papers, but they told me I could not have the ligation immediately since I was getting Medicaid. (My job health insurance didn't start until after a certain amount of time.) On Medicaid, tubal ligations require a 90-day wait while your papers are sent to Sacramento for approval.

Three months later I had the tubal ligation. This time my mother accompanied me because our relationship had improved. I had definite suspicions about the clinic; it gave me an uncomfortable feeling because there were just too many women there. The clinic did nothing but tubals with three of us in a room at a time and the staff literally moving us about on gurneys as if we were on a conveyor belt. The procedure was being done on three different women in the same room, by the same doctor, at the same time. In the hall the gurneys were lined up waiting their turn. Nothing about this situation seemed right: I didn't know the doctor or the anesthesiologist. I didn't know their names, and I doubt if they even knew ours. This was a Medicaid-funded clinic to which I had been referred by Planned Parenthood, so I thought it would be a reputable clinic, but nothing felt right. While I was on the gurney in the hall, I said to one of the nurses rushing by, "Excuse me, I've changed my mind. I think I would like to get another opinion." She claimed it was too late and that the security guards would prevent me from leaving.

Even though I was uncomfortable with the procedures, I figured they probably knew what they were doing and went ahead with it. However, within seven months I was pregnant again. The tubal had failed. When I went back to complain, I found out the clinic had closed. I tried to track it down but found it had gone out of business—although my understanding is that the director of the clinic opened a similar clinic under another name.

I knew I could not handle this new pregnancy. By the time I found out I was pregnant, I had stopped seeing the father because he was abusing drugs and alcohol. He had a lot of problems and definitely was not marriage material.

Being pregnant again was hard to take because I was totally unprepared for this news. During the 90-day waiting period for my tubal ligation, Medicaid people had kept calling to advise me that this procedure was 99.9% effective and that I'd be sterile for the rest of my life. Then I'd signed a stack of papers declaring that I understood this was an irreversible procedure; it would make me sterile for life. No one suggested that a botched job might leave me pregnant in a year. During that waiting period I kept thinking that if I weren't DES, perhaps later I would have wanted another baby. I was only 24, but they approved it because I was low-income and I already had three kids. This reasoning set off alarm bells for me; our being low-income should not have had anything to do with Medicaid approval of my decision. I also felt that the officials were happy to approve of my sterilization because I was a woman of color and they felt there were plenty of little brown babies running around. One of my cousins had been sterilized in Puerto Rico during the mass sterilizations they did in the '70s. You could literally improve your standard of living by having a sterilization because you would get a stipend and be eligible for improved housing and lowered utility bills—if you agreed to be sterilized. It was a big government push.

The week that I found out my tubal had failed, I was in shock. I remember sitting in the clinic office when they told me the pregnancy test was positive. Gabriel was six and the twins were two. I knew immediately that I wanted an abortion. I didn't even have to think about it. I was totally traumatized to realize I was six weeks pregnant. Driving home, I got so depressed that I even thought about killing myself. It would be easy, I thought, to put the kids in the car and drive off the Santa Monica Pier. Then it will all be over and whatever happens to me—if my soul burns in purgatory for all eternity—so be it. A day later I called the clinic back and told them, "You know, I almost killed myself yesterday. I am really desperate to end this pregnancy." They had scheduled me for three days later, but when I told them how desperate I was, they agreed to let me come in that afternoon. I found someone to watch the kids and went in.

After this abortion I was depressed and felt more haunted than after my previous abortion. Perhaps it was because I wasn't as busy—the kids were older and I was going to school full time working on my master's degree in cultural studies with an emphasis on the U.S. and Latin America. Though I was taking a lot of courses, I was only in class three days a week, so I had more time to contemplate. Sometimes I thought that all my negative feelings toward the father had caused me to choose the abortion. When I was rational, I knew that wasn't true. It simply wasn't a good situation in which to bring a child into the world.

After this abortion I went to a support group at the Feminist Health Clinic that used to be on Hollywood Boulevard—one of the first to get firebombed in Los Angeles. The group was very supportive and the members suggested that I go through my gynecologist to have the tubal done the second time. Taking their advice, I went to a private gynecologist and had it done in a real hospital where I stayed overnight. I wish someone had steered me clear of that butcher shop where I'd gone the first time. I would have saved myself so much pain. My gynecologist explained to me why the first tubal had not taken. Essentially the procedure is to cut, tie and then cauterize. Although the first doctor had cut and tied one tube, it was not cauterized and the second Fallopian tube was untouched.

After the second tubal ligation, years passed and I didn't get pregnant. I trusted my doctor and had healed physically, spiritually and emotionally. During this time the Catholic church was not that vocally opposed to abortion. No one preached homilies on the subject, nor was abortion and birth control discussed in church. Everybody was already doing whatever they needed to do to not have 20 or 30 kids, but it was not controversial.

I was coping with life and everything was progressing nicely when my son began taking religious education to make his first communion. Our parish had instituted a parent education program to counteract the habit of many parents who dropped their kids at catechism on Saturday morning, picking them up again and having no further contact with the parish all week. The parents were not taking their kids to mass or going themselves. Since I had been raised that you had to be at death's door to get out of going to church, I had been raising my kids the same way—everywhere we lived, we have *always* gone to church.

The Parent Education Project started well. We met each Thursday evening from seven to nine and helped out one Saturday per month with the catechism classes. It was a caring, warm environment and very spiritual. Lay people taught it and we always lit a candle, read some Scripture, and discussed the topic at hand. We talked about moral issues but not birth control, sexuality or anything of that nature.

I enjoyed these classes and with my strong Scriptural background was frequently the only one who had ever heard the Bible passage being read. I always had a lot to contribute to the class and didn't mind giving up my Thursday nights—even though it wasn't easy to juggle my homework, the class and caring for the children. The course lasted nine months.

The next time around when the twins were preparing to make their sacraments, the class was different. It was organized around two thick books published in Argentina; the English translations we read were simply photocopied and stapled together, without any reference to being a translation or from Argentina. The archdiocese was testing a new program in certain select parishes, and we were the lucky ones. The whole focus of this parent education program was extremely conservative and did not emphasize spiritual or biblical issues. The book made anachronistic assertions like, "In the proper Catholic family the mother stays home and has children and the father goes out to work." This hardly related to my life—or to most Americans today. When I found out that the book was from Argentina, it made sense. From my Latin American studies and travel, I knew that Argentina is not a very healthy place for people of color, for women or for just about anybody except a white male with a lot of European background and money.

The homework for each session was reading followed by a question-and-answer, fill-in-the blank section. I was not pleased with some questions like, "What does your father do for a living?" and "How much money does your father make?" As before, the instructors were lay people, but this time they were extremely right-wing and anti-abortion. They never spent class time discussing the assignments and appeared not to have read them because when I asked specific questions about the readings, they never seemed to know what I was talking about. The instructors would pick a topic—such as gun control, pollution, abortion or the space program—and then lecture us on it for the whole session with no time allotted for class discussion or intervention.

We were about three-quarters through the first book, when one of the two instructors gave us an assignment called something like the "Elizabeth" project. This instructor, a young woman, was active in Operation Rescue and had picketed and blockaded clinics. We were all given the assignment to pick a name from a list and then instructed to pray for this name. Both we parents and our children were supposed to pick a name and pray for this person. When I asked what we were to pray for, I was told, "This name is for the soul of some child that has been aborted." I got up and left.

By this point I had already walked out of class three other times. Once occurred when the same instructor had called pro-choice people murderers; instead of arguing with her, I left to avoid jeopardizing my children's first communion. The second time I walked out, when the topic again was on abortion, two other parents walked out after me. Usually when the instructors took hyper-conservative stands on other issues, I would just bury my head in a book or magazine.

I began going to class, signing my name on the roll sheet, and withholding any participation. I had made it clear that if we were not going to discuss the book, I saw no reason to be there. Attendance was mandatory, however. If we missed more than three classes in a nine-month period, the possibility of our children's taking their sacraments would be severely compromised, they told us. The two parents who had walked out with me told me that they agreed with me but didn't want to say anything because they were not very active in the church. But I *was* active; I was a lector for the masses and a teacher for the children's catechism classes (CCD).

The day after the confrontation over the Elizabeth project, I called the nun who directed the CCD program, explaining the situation to her. She knew that I was finding myself increasingly uncomfortable in this parish because the tenor of the homilies at church had become increasingly anti-abortion. The sister directed me to the main priest, who then gave her the authority to handle the problem. She decided to let me change to a class for confirmation parents, which was being taught by my godfather, a warm and godly man.

Apparently this sister paid a price for being a strong woman and for getting me out of that class; she mysteriously left the parish soon after that, though she was supposed to have stayed for another year. Usually there is a special mass for one of the clergy leaving, with a farewell party, but she was just gone and we weren't told where she went. I am grateful at least that she was there when Jessica and Daniel made their sacrament. Earlier that year I had received some advice to expect repercussions like the sudden departure of this sister. I had attended a vigil sponsored by the Religious Coalition for Abortion Rights where Rosemary Stasek, the executive director of California Catholics for Free Choice, spoke.

During the week of my protest over the Elizabeth project, I called her and she warned me that once it had come to the attention of the parish that I was pro-choice or had pro-choice bumper stickers on my car, I could expect major repercussions just for speaking out on this issue.

Never had I told anyone at church about my abortion experience or even brought it up at confession. I have confessed in my own heart directly to God—just in case. Actually, I kind of felt guilty about confessing, because I don't really think it was a sin. Both abortions took place at six or seven weeks of pregnancy, and as far as I'm concerned, at that stage it's a bunch of cells with no soul. I don't expect to meet it when I go to heaven, so I felt odd confessing, but then I said, "Oh well, better safe than sorry. Just in case I'm wrong, *I confess!*"

At moments like this I almost wished I were a Protestant. Rosemary also pointed out that Episcopal clergy are not opposed to birth control and abortion. But I thought, "For all the things about the Catholic church that I love, and all the things about the Catholic church that I hate, I've *been* a Protestant, and it was like eating diet food. No guilt but just too light!" I went back to church and didn't experience any major problems other than the nun leaving, but gradually, after the twins made their first communion, we started going to another church for mass.

My children and I are moving to northern California soon and I am looking forward to starting over in a new parish. A lot of Catholics encounter problems like this and more or less leave the church. Issues like having to be married in the church (if not, your children are illegitimate and you're an adulterer) or divorce or birth control cause conflict. Of those who remain Catholic, probably 80% just accept those teachings they like and leave the rest behind, ignoring what they can't live with, saying in effect, "I have to do what's best for me." Most women just are not willing to obey all that and have 17 children.

A friend of mine was one of 13 children whose family was dirt poor when they were growing up. His father had to work two jobs just to scrape by. My friend told me, "We were good Catholics and every time my father even looked at my mother, she got pregnant." Ultimately his mother died an alcoholic. She explained that she turned to alcohol because her husband despised drinking and if she had alcohol on her breath, he wouldn't come near her. That was her birth control, but she ended up an alcoholic and drank herself to death in order to obey the rules of her church—a total tragedy.

This attitude of quietly circumventing church prohibitions prevails among Catholics. As for me, I've been taking my children since they were in strollers to pro-choice demonstrations and to clinic defenses. Now that they're older I've explained to them a little more of what it's all about. My mother handed on to me both her faith and her pro-choice attitudes and I am passing them on to my children.

Part 2

Other Perspectives §

14

In Memory of Marie: Abortion in Earlier Days §

Betty Hadden

When I was nine, my grandmother told me we were going to Marie's house. Marie was 15, and she was dead. We dressed in our Sunday best and walked in warm sunshine the short block separating Marie's home from ours in that small Kentucky town. A member of the family met us at the door. There were a few people standing about the room conversing in low tones and whispers. Following my grandmother, I moved toward the casket placed along a wall of the living room.

Marie lay there, so quiet. Marie, who had always been the vivacious one, laughing and smiling, walking at a fast clip with black curls bouncing about her face. She was so beautiful that the little girls in my class stared at her, longing for the day when they too would be grown like Marie. Now we stood before the casket, Grandmother Ida holding my hand. The rigid repose on Marie's face amazed me, but my eyes were diverted, riveted to the great abdomen that extended up from her small body.

Later Grandmother Ida, who raised my sister and me and who always had time for our questions, explained in her direct manner that Marie, though unmarried, had loved a man and conceived their child. Grandmother did not know the circumstances leading to the death of Marie and the child within her. I was too young to ask why the two doctors in town had not helped her or why she had not gone to the hospital, 25 miles away.

I suspect that my grandmother, who read both the local paper and the *Louisville Courier Journal,* knew all about Margaret Sanger. Only 16 years earlier Sanger and her sister had been harassed (principally by religious organizations) and jailed for their efforts to disseminate birth control information. When I was older and learned that contraceptive information had been suppressed for centuries, I was angry and thought of Marie. Even though the condom had been introduced in England in 1680, the cruel censorship of birth control information caused women of child-bearing age to die needlessly over the centuries.

I never escaped the memory of Marie's casket. As I was growing up, I would wonder about sex, birth and death. During long summer evenings spent in the porch swing and winter months beside the fireplace, I questioned Grandmother Ida about pregnancy and motherhood. She was decisive and outspoken in her opinion that a woman should make the decision about the number of children she would bear and that consideration should be given to the mother's health, the amount of time that could be spent with the children, and the economic resources available.

Grandmother practiced what she preached. In 1909 she announced to my grandfather she was having no more children. Though primitive by today's standards, contraceptive and abortion knowledge was shared by women in their extended circles of family and friends. Two of grandmother's sisters had only one child and another had no children. I wish I had known to ask my grandmother what she thought of Sanger and the Comstock Law. I do know that it never seemed to have crossed her mind that birth control was anything other than a woman's business. My grandfather concurred and thus it was that my sister and I grew up in a feminist Christian home (an oxymoron at that time). It was many years before we became aware that anyone separated the values we were raised by and considered them contradictory.

In 1931, two years after Marie's death, Grandmother Ida's niece, a student at a distant college, unexpectedly came to our home. Evelyn was very ill and had sought help and understanding where she knew it was available. Through wisdom and knowledge passed down through generations of women, grandmother had become a capable nurse and was the doctor and nurse for our family—and sometimes the whole neighborhood.

Putting Evelyn to bed, Grandmother Ida went to work, delegating part of the care to me. My questions started anew at the sight of so much blood, and it was then I learned about abortion. Grandmother said that both kitchen-table abortions and those performed by a doctor (for women who had money) were frequent. Through Grandmother Ida's care and God's grace, Evelyn recovered. She stayed with us a week until she had gained back her strength. This young Christian woman remained an active member of the church her entire life and many people, including me, benefitted from her care and her concern for those in need.

When I was thirteen and my sister was ten, we moved north across the Mason-Dixon Line to live in Indiana with our mother who had recently remarried. Although I loved my grandparents dearly, I wanted to be with mom. We had been separated for seven years, ever since my grandparents had learned of the abuse and neglect all three of us had endured from my father. They had urged Mom to get a divorce and promised to care for my sister and me until we no longer needed supervision. My parents were divorced in 1926 and never once did my father attempt to see us or contribute anything financially for our support.

After settling into our new home with Mom and her new husband in 1933, my sister and I worked hard to take care of ourselves. After Mom went to work in the morning, we prepared our food, arrived at school on time, made good grades, cleaned the house and kept coal in the furnace. Mom was always at work. Like so many uneducated, unskilled young women at that time, she had found employment in the mills, but her wages were meager. Often there wasn't enough for food and rent.

Soon a new factor made Mom's circumstances desperate. Like many other women down through the ages (as described by Edward Shorter in *A History of Women's Bodies),* Mom now faced both poverty and pregnancy. Since her husband was often unemployed, it was necessary for her to work in order to survive. Jobs were still scarce and tenuous as the country struggled with the great Depression.

Mom decided to risk a self-induced abortion. At that time drugs were available having "an emmenagogue power." Unlike my grandmother, Mom did not talk to me but lay quietly in bed. I did what I was asked to do and what I thought would be helpful, but essentially Mom recovered with only the attention of a 13-year-old child. Dealing with this crisis seemed very natural, however, after having listened to my grandmother's conversations with her friends. I had often preferred being inside with their stories to being outside with other children. These older women, ages ranging from 50 to 80, broached any topic, seemingly unaffected by my presence. They talked about their children and gardens, preserving food, about sickness and remedies, about birth and abortion. I had learned that the only attendant at the birth of my grandmother's children was her mother ... that Lillian had self-aborted with a hat pin ... that a doctor had told one woman another pregnancy would kill her. Caring for my mother after her abortion seemed natural in this context.

Life went on and I continued to listen, but now it was my mother and her friends, all in their 30s and working in the mills. They talked about their jobs, money, cheap rent, food bargains, pregnancy, contraception, abortion and divorce. They lived from paycheck to paycheck. A missed one was a crisis—and we were evicted for nonpayment of rent during a strike at the mills.

From these younger women, I learned that husbands did not want any more children, but that the responsibility for not having children belonged to the woman. (That is why the first question Margaret Sanger directed at women when she began her crusade was, "Do you want any more children?") Tearfully my aunt told her story: her husband had said that if she became pregnant again, he would leave her. She became pregnant so she had an abortion. When economic times were a bit better, one of my mother's friends was able to have an abortion performed by a doctor. Others followed. These two generations of women, in whose company I grew up, lived at what would now be called the poverty level. They were all God-fearing, hard-working and law-abiding—except in the matter of those relatively recent laws passed against abortion.

Doctors' fees for illegal abortions varied considerably. In the late '40s, a friend of my mother paid $400. Someone else I heard about paid $500 in a doctor's office in the '50s. Now we can pick up a magazine at the drug store and find information about contraception and abortion, but in my youth this information had to be passed from person to person.

Prominent doctors have discussed the abortions they performed before it was legalized. Dr. Robert Spencer admitted before his death in 1969 that he had probably performed 75,000 abortions in 60 years of practice. Furthermore, he knew other doctors in New York, Texas and Maryland who had long been performing abortion as an act of conscience. "Once I realized that a woman should be the dictator of what went on in her own body, I just set out to help," Spencer declared. This realization came to him in 1923 when a miner's wife asked for an abortion, saying she had difficulty feeding the four children she already had. Performing abortions out of this conviction, Spencer charged from $50 to $100 for each one.

Now I am old and the women I listened to in my youth sleep in their graves. Still this issue concerns me. I think of St. Thomas Aquinas who promised women that taking the vows to become a nun would be a means of escaping the disabilities of a woman's sex and the horrors of pregnancy and childbirth. I also think of a congressman's opposition to Medicaid funding of abortion for poor women and girl children, pregnant by rape and incest. His only concern is "the unwanted, innocently inconvenient unborn." What will the future hold for these poor girls forced to complete pregnancies begun in violence?

The continuous efforts to restrict abortion today angers me. I think of my grandmother, an equal partner in marriage, helping to ease the desperation of poverty-stricken, unwillingly pregnant women. She led a long, happy life—but her country did not allow her to vote until she was 48 years old. I think of my mother's short, difficult life and Margaret Sanger, my hero. I always smile when remembering the young woman who rejected Franklin Roosevelt's proposal of marriage; he stipulated that he would require six children and she retorted, "I am not a cow."

I think of my mother-in-law, in poor health and economic distress, who resorted to abortions after the birth of her third child. Her husband blamed her for getting pregnant every time they had intercourse and told her that *he* couldn't afford any more children. I recall a friend who went to Mexico in 1970 for an illegal but clean and safe abortion. Then 1973 came and abortion was legal in the U.S., but in Mexico significant numbers of women still die every year from the effects of illegal abortions.

My mood darkens remembering 1980—the year two young women, my niece and the daughter of a friend, were raped. In the same year my church, the Southern Baptist Convention, passed a resolution against abortion, even in the instance of pregnancy resulting from rape. Being with these young women during this year, I observed that the one who was unchurched made a better recovery from rape: she was angry and indignant and, in an effort to prevent the rape of other women, gave a series of interviews to the newspaper. My niece, on the other hand, in church all her life, was ashamed because she had been raped. Knowing the stigma attached to a woman who had been raped in her Southern community, she at first planned to leave town secretly. Fearful of losing the protection of her family, however, after four days she finally talked to her mother and was soon given the medical and legal help available to the affluent. Discreet police made no record of the crime after interrogating the rapist, a well-known local resident, who confessed. Despite his daughter's experience, my niece's father continued to make large contributions to Swaggart, Falwell, Bakker and Robertson—men who oppose legal abortions even for rape victims. As for me, I can no longer attend the Southern Baptist Church—with its stance against abortion for rape victims—or indeed any of the churches in my community.

My mood brightens with thoughts of two men friends, one the father of one child, the other of two, who agreed with their wives that they wanted no more children—and assumed that responsibility. How rare. Generally men regard birth control as a woman's business, but men in power control birth control. I value writers like C.S. Lewis who show compassion on this subject. When asked about contraception, Lewis said he could not comment since nature had denied him any knowledge of the pain and danger of giving birth. Another English writer has said that all the progress of the centuries would be dwarfed on the day that contraception could be planned.

When I hear people deplore the number of abortions performed today, I doubt there are any more happening now than before 1973. For centuries there has been a network of underground abortions around the world. Yet, as various groups work to chip away at the abortion rights gained in 1973, I worry for our daughters. My prayer for my own daughter is that if she becomes a mother, it will be her decision, not that of the church or the government. I remember the past—so many mothers, like my mother, raising their children with no sharing of joy and labor by the father. I pray that the past will not be repeated in the future.

15

Women's Wisdom,
Women's Lore §

Anna McD. Miller

Women's wisdom, women's lore:
women's woes and joys
survival skills, supportive listening
analysis, assessment
prescription and perspective:
the psychology and sociology,
the mythology and mysticism
of being female
passed among the generations
of women in my family
while they worked together
in the kitchen.
And the men taught the boys
"Don't bother the womenfolk
when they're gossiping."

W e were left to ourselves at family festivals—usually in the kitchen or sometimes in my aunt's bedroom when our grandmother, Amy McDonnell West, needed to lie down. We gathered around her, sitting on the bed or the floor to continue the conversations vital to our lives as women, as followers of Christ. Grandmothers, great-grandmothers, aunts and cousins; sisters and sisters-in-law—we all traveled up and down the California coast to visit and help with new babies, to give respite to one caring for an elderly relative or to another who had a teenager in need of a change in environment. And always there were the nurturing, healing, helpful conversations.

We were devout, loving Christian women, concerned about our families and our world. Educationally, some were graduates of universities, others were Bible-college trained, and some had only limited opportunities for formal learning. Among us were Sunday school teachers, church musicians, a missionary, a minister, a minister's wife, a Gospel broadcaster and other women active in their churches. Also dearly loved and accepted in the group were one who attended a liberal church, one who held fundamentalist doctrines but never attended any church at all, and one who married a Buddhist. There was even the woman rancher who didn't believe in a personal God but whose mystical relationship to the land and to her animals brought us renewal and peace and joy in creation whenever we visited her ranch.

Our conversations were a marvelous mix of feminine spirituality, family loyalty, unity in diversity and freedom through strength. These talks reflected our deepest needs, our commitment to stand by one another. They initiated the young, taught traditions to the newly married, supported the middle-aged, and comforted the elderly. We talked about God, creation, people, ethics: women's words, women's wisdom.

Finally being admitted into their conversations gave young

women a strong sense of being initiated into a special tribe: good women who made good decisions about their lives within their own circumstances; strong women who dealt in truth and shielded one another from oppression and the rejection of the wider society—especially the evangelical milieu. Through our family mythology we came to believe in hope and renewal, pilgrimage and Providence, God and ourselves.

I remember longing to be part of these special conversations. One Fourth of July my older sister was asked to help in the kitchen, and I missed her company among the gamboling young cousins. "What do they talk about?" I wondered, calculating about two more years until I would get to join them. But the next year my youngest aunt showed me the cupboard in her bathroom where the Kotex was kept and then sat down on the edge of the bathtub, lit a cigarette and began to talk to me about becoming a "young lady." I had become one of the womenfolk and was given a place in the kitchen to listen, learn and go forth strengthened in my pilgrimage in the world.

There was a strong sense of secrets: we, the initiates, knew the secrets of our foremothers. The joy of being related to those daring, courageous and audacious women was exhilarating. The context of that joy was a relationship to a God who understood us, was for us, and gave us supernatural strength and endurance—a God who was caring, daring, audacious: feminine. For us, God was never exclusively male. At a young age I learned that Jesus had taught that in heaven the male/female division of humanity would be transcended. If we were destined to transcend gender, how much more then did the great and caring God of the universe transcend the temporal categories of gender?

To the men who came through the kitchen for a cup of coffee

or a piece of pie, our conversations might sound like gossip: who was having a baby, getting married or divorced, who was going to a rest home. But for us, the wisdom of the world of women was joyfully and solemnly being transmitted. For what is life but birth and death, relationships, the land and the animals ... and God? These are the things that philosophers and theologians, psychologists and sociologists talk about.

Christian standards also figured in—about premarital sex and what now is called date rape—long before the media named it. Biblical norms for behavior were not seen as arbitrary rules, but as guidelines to enable Christians to live creative lives free of some of the pain involved in broken relationships. Loving, accepting, forgiving, restoring—these were active verbs lived out among family members who realized they themselves were not yet perfect; as a result, they had room in their hearts to forgive as they had been forgiven. Each woman in the family was respected for her own story, and these stories were told with zest, with joy, with sadness, anger or hilarity. There was so much laughter, smoothing the way, creating community; there was so much wisdom and caring and forgiveness.

In this context I learned that my grandmother, Amy McDonnell West, had gone through two abortions early in this century. Failing in health of mind and body due to yearly pregnancies, she made a choice to care for the four children she already had, each spaced a year apart, and to maintain her physical and mental health. Her decision was always related as one of the sad stories, one of the courageous stories. Descended from Scotch-Irish Presbyterians, Amy was raised on the East coast of the U.S. where her father was a pastor. The family placed a high value on education, and Amy attended seminary to prepare as a missionary. When her father took a call to a church in Kansas, Amy accompanied her family and began training as a midwife, traveling from farm to farm assisting an older woman who was knowledgeable about women's problems and childbirth.

In Kansas Amy met and married Nathaniel West, a young farmer who decided that he could make a better living farming in California. In 1909 they packed up their few household goods, their two children and took the train to Sacramento. Though the West family had relatives already settled in northern California, life was hard for the young couple trying to establish a farm in a new territory. They were isolated, far from medical care and churches. Amy, always ready to reach out to those in need, took up her midwifery with the neighboring women. She was always welcome at the farms and ranches and she gradually grew into the role of rural wise woman, dispensing medical aid and advice and becoming a spiritual care giver in the life-and-death situations of people bereft of religious institutions.

Even as a teenager, Amy had never been robust in health. Her frail constitution and thyroid problems caused her to collapse at age 28 just as she was beginning her fifth pregnancy in five years. Her mother came to care for the four preschool children and they talked together about her illness and her options for the future. Well-educated in anatomy and physiology and understanding sterile techniques, Amy decided that she must risk ending the pregnancy herself. Convinced that she could not live through a fifth pregnancy and childbirth, she saw abortion as her only option. With the mental and emotional numbness that comes to those on the edge of survival, Amy sterilized a graduated set of knitting needles and managed to accomplish a very primitive and dangerous medical procedure. Her recovery was slow due to her poor health, but she did not have an infection, so her progress was steady.

Dear grandmother with her web of Victorian contradictions! Though she was strong enough to decide on abortion, she adhered to the prevailing taboos that kept her from discussing her situation with her husband. She also could not discuss with him the only method of birth control available to them—abstinence—so the next year found her pregnant again. Finally she gathered the courage to discuss with him their mutual difficulty. This time they were able to decide together that her health would not survive another pregnancy and childbirth. Rather than risk her death in childbirth, they opted for her second abortion. This time they made a commitment to abstinence because even though they had heard of primitive kinds of diaphragms and condoms, the only reliable method was abstinence. There would be no more pregnancies until her health was recovered.

Three years passed and Amy grew strong. In 1916, aged 32, she bore another child—the first of an additional set of four children. Amy and Nathaniel were considered pillars of faith in their community. Nathaniel continued to farm and Amy became a rural missionary for a small Holiness denomination. She established two churches in northern California, one of which is still a thriving congregation where one of her granddaughters is a member. With eight children, nine grandchildren and eleven great-grandchildren, Amy McDonnell West was the matriarch of the family and the saint of the several surrounding communities.

Whenever the difficult part of Amy's story was told, it was always with a sense of grief—not of condemnation. We all knew that abortion was a desperate measure and very dangerous. Yet we were thankful that our dear grandmother, full of fun and the spirit of Christ, had survived to share with us God's love. When we heard the stories of other missionary women who died from annual pregnancies and overwork, we were grateful that she had chosen to regain her mental and physical health to raise those four children and the four that followed later. We thanked God that she could contribute to the lives of her grandchildren and great-grandchildren, who learned of the love of God and the power of prayer from their saintly great-grammy. Her Christian influence extended beyond her own family because of her missionary labors. Who knows how many people have found Christ through her? Surely God guided her efforts at family planning and preserving her own health so that she could be God's instrument in the world.

In our sharing in the kitchen, we admired Grandmother's courage, grieving that such decisions are sometimes necessary in a world fallen from the grace God wishes for it. Grandmother was surely not condemned as a sinner for those abortions. Neither was the aunt who became pregnant out of wedlock. The family rallied to help this aunt keep her baby. Nor did the family condemn the cousin who was living with her common-law husband. She was loved and accepted, and her companion came with her to family gatherings where he was accepted among the uncles and brothers without comment or raised eyebrows.

I have lived long enough now to have seen many of these people live to the end of their stories. They have committed their lives to Christ, shared the gospel and grown in grace— because they were loved and accepted and encouraged to press on in their best hopes and dreams and endeavors. When I was young, no one called this approach to Christian family life "situation ethics." It was simply a living-out of Christian love and acceptance. Knowing the human frame, remembering that we are dust, believing that God gives us forgiveness and new life through the death and resurrection of Jesus Christ, we dare to forgive and accept one another. Certainly all sin is grievous, but no sin is worse than any other. All sins are forgiven through the suffering of Christ, and all brokenness will one day be restored by the redeeming love of Christ.

Women's wisdom, women's lore. To be taught philosophy and psychology, history and sociology, theology and ethics from such great women in such a humble setting is a marvelous heritage to share with my daughters, my husband and my son.

Because of the conversations that surrounded me, I grew up knowing that being a woman was wonderful and that I would be affirmed. I knew that no matter what the future held or what my struggles might be, I would always find among these women love, understanding, acceptance. I knew this because I had experienced their love for those who were ahead of me and heard their words of understanding, analysis, absolution. My sisters, my aunts, my cousins: all had been affirmed and congratulated for their strength under trial, all had been given credit for their good intentions, for growing in grace. I matured knowing in my heart I would receive the same Christian love.

16

Being a Christian and a Clinic Escort §

Sally Carpenter

In 1989 when I escorted at an abortion clinic, I often felt caught between the Christian anti-choice protestors and the other escorts, who were pro-choice feminists and rejected all forms of so-called patriarchal religion. Even though I see things in the feminist movement that bother me as a Christian, I also cringe at the misogyny promoted by fundamentalist churches. Finding a common ground between Christianity and feminism has been difficult at times, particularly during the year I served as an escort.

When I attended my first *Roe* v. *Wade* anniversary pro-choice march in January, 1989, I was 31 years old and the abortion issue meant nothing to me. I didn't even know the term "pro-choice." Like most people who have never experienced an unwanted pregnancy, I didn't think about abortion. Before moving to Fort Wayne, Indiana, I had studied at a seminary, but the issue was never discussed. The student body was active on certain social issues, but legalized abortion (whether pro or con) was not one of them. Once I heard a female seminarian say, "I don't see how anyone could ever have an abortion!" and nobody argued with her.

My participation in the pro-choice march was motivated by boredom and restlessness as much as by a desire to be of service. I had thought about getting involved in some kind of cause, but I didn't know which one. Having been too young in the '60s to participate in the peace movement, I looked forward to attending a real political march. I didn't attend the anti-choice march held the same day because the newspaper letters to the editor with "pro-life" views seemed too cold, uncaring and judgmental; one letter even said that any woman who died from an illegal abortion deserved to die.

One woman speaker at the post-march rally asked for volunteers to assist clients entering the Women's Health Organization, the only women's health care facility performing abortions in northeastern Indiana. First trimester abortions are performed at this clinic by an out-of-city physician (any local doctor doing abortions would be blackballed by the community in Fort Wayne, known as "the city of churches"). As coördinator of clinic defense, this woman arranged for escorts to help those with appointments get past the anti-abortion protestors. The escorts, both men and women, were volunteers with no official connection to the clinic. From her speech, escorting sounded like an exciting kind of service: necessary, different, dangerous and more stimulating than stuffing envelopes. As a Christian I also felt an obligation to work for justice and equality.

After I had signed up for the escort training session, I

realized that I first needed to learn about abortion and to resolve whether my Christian values were compatible with assisting an organization that, according to some, "killed babies." I searched the public library for information on abortion. At first I was ambivalent and did much soul-searching, since up to then the *only* Christian view I knew was against abortion. To my relief I located some material presenting the Christian pro-choice position. I didn't know what stance the mainline denominations had on abortion. I found that the anti-choice Christian position is more widely published. In fact, I have yet to see a Christian bookstore carry even one pro-choice book. Months later I discovered the Religious Coalition for Abortion Rights and was delighted to read its well-written, religiously oriented pro-choice literature. The average layperson, however, must put out a dedicated effort to find such material.

My first escort experience was on a chilly Saturday in late February. Like everyone else, I layered myself in warm clothes for my lengthy stay outdoors. That first day I mostly observed, preparing for a more active role in following weeks. The clinic's location in downtown Fort Wayne renders the building vulnerable to the protestors who come on the once-a-week "procedure days" (when abortions are performed). The Women's Health Organization had tried to move the clinic, housed in a remodeled old brownstone, to a better location, but landlords would not rent to a group providing abortions among other services. Since the clinic has no private parking area, clients and staff park nearby and have to cross a busy street to the clinic, which is surrounded by public sidewalks where protesters can gather.

On most procedure days a dozen or so escorts plus 30 to 60 anti-choice protestors assembled. During the months I served as an escort, I became familiar with the protestors, all faithful church attenders and absolutely sincere about their beliefs. They included Catholics, Missouri Synod Lutherans, Pentecostals, members of independent fundamentalist churches and students from the local Bible college. All the anti-choice leaders were white, male clergy. (A year later one of these pastors was arrested and convicted of punching an escort in the face as she helped a woman into the clinic.) Among the Catholics were parochial students bussed in to participate. One of the fundamentalist leaders persuaded his youth group to cut their public school classes in order to march at the clinic—but admonished them not to tell their parents.

On a typical day most of the protestors slowly circled the sidewalk in front of the clinic in a "Jericho Prayer March" (in hopes that the clinic's walls would come tumbling down). Grim-faced, these marchers carried signs: "Abortion Stops a Heartbeat," "Big Bucks for Little Doctors," "The Womb Is the Tomb," and "Equal Rights for Unborn Women." Once I asked the man carrying this sign if he believed in equal rights for women already born; he said nothing. The protestors also held posters of bright-eyed, smiling babies (always Caucasian) or full-color blow ups of bloody "aborted fetuses"—which often turn out to be actually pictures of miscarriages or stillbirths.

Parents made their young children march for hours, often in rain or cold weather. Mothers pushed strollers with babies so that a client would see the babies and perhaps decide to complete her pregnancy. The marchers loudly recited "prayer litanies" that condemned the "Satanic clinic staff who shed innocent blood," and the "deathscorts who drag women to the slaughterhouse." They also sang hymns and when a client approached would start a loud rendition of "Jesus Loves the Little Children." Protestors often blocked the sidewalk with showy "prayer circles," apparently unaware of Jesus' words about prayer on street corners: "And when you pray, you must not be like the hypocrites; for they love to stand in the synagogues and at the street corners, that they may be seen by men" (Mt 6:5).

Most aggressive and frightening were the protestors called "street counselors" who stood poised by the parking lots as a last-ditch, one-on-one effort to persuade clients, with force if necessary, into changing their minds. These counselors would run up to a client's car and follow her elbow-to-elbow all the way to the clinic door, talking non-stop and shoving into her hands brochures and three-inch plastic fetus dolls. The brochures said things like, "Most women only have one opportunity to get pregnant; don't kill the only baby you'll every have." These counselors would shout a variety of slogans into the client's ear: "Don't kill your baby," "Your baby has a heartbeat," "Jesus loves your baby," "Just give us five minutes of your time," and "Mommy, don't kill me." If a client plowed past this abuse and through the lines of marchers, she was again greeted by counselors on leaving the clinic: "How do you feel now that you've killed your baby?"

Such antics performed by so-called Christians shocked and nauseated me. Such harassment is contrary to the spirit of Christianity, so I was astonished these people, who seemed well-read in the Bible, could pervert God's love in this way. Jesus never used behavior like this but always treated women with dignity and gentleness. Neither Jesus nor the disciples forced people against their wills. One reason I escorted was to demonstrate that not *all* Christians are bullies.

Escorting was physically and emotionally exhausting. On the procedure days, when my work schedule permitted, I came to the clinic before seven in the morning and stayed until the last client arrived around noon. To distinguish ourselves from the protestors, we escorts wore handmade vests with "ESCORT" blazoned on the front and back. We stood waiting for clients in bitter cold and snow, in rain and in summer heat. The long stretches of waiting could be boring, and the sidewalk was hard on the feet. Listening for hours to the protestors' singing and the street counselors' shouting roiled our nerves. After escorting I was always ready for a long nap.

Our strategy as escorts was to watch each approaching car for possible clients so we could reach the client's car ahead of the street counselors. An escort then asked the client if she wanted assistance. Usually the woman took one glance at the mob blocking the building and agreed. The escorts then held hands or more often put their arms on the shoulders of the next escort, forming a tight circle around the woman and her companions. We moved as quickly as a mass of people can, with only our bodies between the client and the truculent counselors. To drown out the counselors we talked to the client, sang songs or distracted the counselors with one-on-one debates. Some escorts even warded off pugnacious counselors by leaping about like a basketball guard. We also intercepted the brochures and fetus dolls.

Our presence provoked these Christian counselors—so that they became even less loving and more violent. Often I saw them kick, trip, shove, elbow, pinch and even spit on the escorts— supposedly in the service of Jesus Christ. If an escort grabbed a brochure, the counselors would complain loudly to the police. Once a student at a Bible college viciously screamed at me for "stealing" a pamphlet a client didn't want. The student's unblinking eyes glared at me in hate. Annoyed, I screamed back and she threatened to have me arrested. Once as I brought in a client, another counselor pushed against me so roughly that I almost fell over. However, if an escort accidentally brushed against one of the protestors, they would immediately complain to the police and want that escort arrested for assault. One counselor actually performed a "citizen's arrest" against an escort, but the court later dropped the charge.

We escorts tried to remain calm, but as a typical morning wore on and the counselors grew more aggressive, tempers flared and some escorts would yell back at the protestors to shut up and go away. Some even used profanity. Occasionally escorts stopped potential fights between the clients and the protestors, who would provoke boyfriends and fathers until they almost came to blows. To intimidate clients, the anti-abortion demonstrators often used cameras to take their pictures. To counter this picture-taking, escorts brought towels or sheets and offered to cover the client's face if she wanted privacy. Unfortunately, this effort added anxiety because the woman couldn't see through the towel. She was forced to cling to her companion or to an escort, trusting that we took her to the correct place.

As a Christian, I thought I could discuss these issues with the protestors, but they were unwilling to listen to anyone who did not agree with them. They couldn't believe that a Christian would participate in escorting women seeking an abortion. I told one counselor that for many centuries the Catholic church *did* allow abortion up to the time of "quickening." The woman gave me a startled look and asked what my sources were for that statement. When I said I had read it in a book at the public library, she scoffed, "A person can write anything in a book."

As escorts, we had little time to get to know the clients, but I did hear a few stories of why these women needed abortions. A married woman and her husband said they already had several children and couldn't afford another. Another client had faithfully used birth control, but it had failed. One day I talked with the parents of a 14-year-old teenager who said their daughter was pregnant from a much older, no-good boyfriend. Then the boyfriend arrived and tried to get inside the clinic, presumably to stop the abortion. We did not let him in and he waited for a long time on the sidewalk.

Some stories were not so simple. One woman told us that when she was a teenager, she had given birth to a baby girl who was taken away for adoption. She had deeply mourned the loss of that child, so she kept the baby of her second unplanned pregnancy, a boy. Angry at not having a girl, the woman had abused her baby. Eventually she sought professional help for her abusiveness. Now she was pregnant a third time and had decided that she couldn't deal with the pain of adoption again, nor could she risk abusing another child.

Did the counselors ever convince a woman not to have an abortion? No. Instead, their harassment caused many clients to cry, to grow more nervous, to become hysterical, or to faint. One client clutched my arm in a tight grip and did not let go until we were inside the clinic's waiting room, where she gave me a soft, heartfelt "thank you." The behavior of the protestors infuriated me so much that, after escorting, my anger didn't dissipate for at least a day. I was angry at them for demonstrating so much hate against women in God's name. It felt as though the protestors were making a public mockery of my deep beliefs.

I was upset not only at the anti-choice churches but at the mainline churches for their failure to stand up for abortion rights and to condemn the clinic harassment. I wanted to talk to other Christians about the abortion issue and recruit more escorts, but few people were interested. Sometimes I felt like the only pro-choice Christian in town.

While I became friendly with most of the escorts and found them to be good and honorable people, almost none of them were Christians. Some were openly hostile toward all forms of religion, especially Christianity. Some of the most intelligent and well-educated escorts turned highly emotional on the subject of religion, condemning all aspects of religion as bad and oppressive. This "religion bashing" made me uncomfortable—especially during the weekly escort meetings held to plan strategy, to encourage and to provide a safe forum to vent the anger built up during escorting.

Insults about "the Christians" often ran on without resolution or healing, and the phrase "the church" was used as if all churches were like these people. At times I calmly reminded the others that not all Christians are like the protestors, but the insults continued. After a time the religion bashing irked me so much that I wrote a letter to all our escorts expressing my discomfort. Several escorts apologized to me for any offense they had caused—but the insults never completely disappeared.

One incident stands out as an example of the discomfort I felt as a Christian. Some protestors outside the clinic were reading loudly from the Bible. To me it seemed the counselor's purpose here was not devotional but an attempt to annoy the escorts. To counter, some escorts began reading pro-choice material aloud to drown out the Bible readers. I felt torn; while I did not appreciate the show the counselors made of reading the Bible, I also felt uneasy at the escorts trying to drown out the Bible-readers while other escorts made fun of the Bible reading.

In 1989 the Women's Health Organization in Fort Wayne was further tormented by three assaults from Operation Rescue, a group founded by Randall Terry. On each occasion demonstrators used forcible blockades to prevent women from entering the clinic. Terry, a New York used-car salesman-turned-evangelist, invented this tactic. He reasoned that closing down clinics for a day by blockade would produce two results: in the short run, some women would carry their pregnancies to term; in the long run, the courts would be so swamped with mass arrests that abortion laws would be repealed. In some cities, clinics hit by Operation Rescue simply rescheduled appointments, but in Fort Wayne the clinic never closed. Escorts helped the clients wait until the arrests of protestors were completed.

The first Operation Rescue attack on the Fort Wayne clinic was set for a date in March that was kept secret even from the participants. Local fundamentalist churches hosted training sessions to which the media and escorts were denied admittance. Still, the escorts learned the date from an anti-choice hot line, so we were notified the night before. I was so nervous and worried that I hardly slept that night. The next morning as I parked my car at dawn and walked quietly to the clinic in the chilly air, I felt rather bulky in my several layers of clothing. None of our 50 escorts knew the exact time of the "hit," so we waited, anxiety growing. We heard rumors that up to a thousand protestors might come. Several cars drove by slowly while the drivers checked out the territory.

A little after six, the report came, "The Christians are

coming!'' We sprang into action. We had constructed four-foot high plywood barricades to keep the OR people as far from the building as possible, since in other cities, OR protestors had actually entered clinics to harass staff and vandalize equipment. We now set up those barricades, forming a wall around the front lawn, each piece of plywood held up by an escort.

Over a hundred protestors, looking tired and grumpy from an all-night prayer vigil and fast, walked from their buses. They seemed annoyed by the barricades, but taking out homemade mats, they sat down in several rows along our wall. Those protestors who did not want to be arrested stood in the park beside our building as "prayer warriors" to lend support and sing hymns. We waited, wondering what the protestors would do next. Meanwhile the clinic administrator phoned the police.

The police had already been alerted because OR leaders always meet with police beforehand to discuss how arrests will be handled, hoping to strike deals so the arrests can be stretched out as long as possible. By delaying arrests, OR can keep a clinic closed longer and discourage incoming clients. Soon 60 uniformed police arrived and sealed off the block with orange sawhorses so that only those with escort vests were allowed in. Meanwhile television cameras, radio microphones and reporters from all the media in the city began arriving. The police chief used a bullhorn to communicate to the protestors, and the escorts used walkie talkies to notify each other of approaching clients. An ambulance stood by for injuries. The air was thick with tension.

In a few minutes the chief of police arrived and announced to the protestors they had ten minutes to disperse or arrests would commence. Just then the first client arrived with a woman friend, and the escorts sprang to action. In other cities, the escorts had lifted women over the seated protestors and into the building, so we planned to try this same tactic. Because of the television cameras, we covered both women's faces with towels. Forming a tight circle around both women, we shuffled across the street toward the barricades like a giant centipede. According to the national OR rules, "rescuers" are not to stand up, talk to anyone (especially escorts or reporters) or react to events around them, but our local protestors ignored their mandate and rose up, linking arms and shouting, "Jesus loves you! Don't kill your baby!"

Our tight ball of escorts shoved against the protestors who pushed back. The police chief ordered us to back off, or we too would be arrested. Frustrated, we returned to our starting place. At this point we realized that we needed a place for the women to wait until the ordeal was over, so we put them in a van parked nearby. As the morning wore on, street counselors tried to hold up their "bloody fetus" pictures to the van windows. The clinic sent one of its genuine counselors to sit in the van and talk with the clients.

Meanwhile, the arrests had begun. Despite the large number of officers present, they made arrests only one at a time. The protestors went limp in passive resistance and four officers were needed (one holding each limb) to carry them to a waiting bus. Some protestors refused to board the bus and had to be carried on, later complaining of "rough handling."

When the clinic nurses arrived, we were determined to get at least one nurse inside. By now many bystanders had arrived to watch the show, lined up behind the police barricades. As escorts, we circled one nurse and moved to the side of the plywood wall beside several low-hanging trees. The protestors once more stood up and pushed us. An officer ordered the protestors to back off, but they refused. In spite of this we successfully lifted a nurse over the protestors' heads and she was grabbed by the escorts behind the barricades. The police chief shouted at us, "If you do that again, I'll have you arrested for disorderly conduct." He seemed more eager to arrest the escorts than the protestors.

Strangely enough, some of the more vocal and aggressive street counselors were not among the lawbreakers, but rather stood among the prayer warriors, as far away from the police as possible. More than three hours after the first arrests, the police finally cleared away all the sit-down protestors and drove the 106 lawbreakers to the city armory for processing and release. With the sidewalk clear, we acted quickly to get women into the clinic before the prayer warriors decided to perform a second sit-in. I felt immense pride that day for doing the important work of keeping the clinic open. The protestors—who had set out to oppress women seeking abortions—had been defeated. At one point I heard a bystander call out, "Thank you, escorts!" Such expressions of appreciation were frequent on a regular day of escorting but were especially welcome on this day.

By noon I was exhausted. All clients scheduled for abortions that day were inside the clinic, and the doctor had been able to get in too. The national OR leaders were upset that Northeast Indiana Rescue had failed to close down the clinic for the whole day, so the local protestors were under pressure to try again.

When the second "rescue" came in June, we knew the date ahead of time an put up the wall again. The police arrived early this time and constructed police barricades, stringing yellow tape around the clinic entrance. We were surprised to see the protestors arrive and walk along the sidewalk in their usual

Jericho march, so we wondered if we had the date wrong.

Then just at eight, while several escorts were walking in a client, the anti-choice leader shouted, "Now!" and the marchers climbed over the police barricades, breaking them down, in order once again to sit along our makeshift wall. An officer told us later that usually anyone crossing a police line is immediately arrested or even deterred by shooting, but the police took no such action against these protestors. The legs of the escorts and the client were pinned by a sea of sit-down protestors. Those trapped were forced to step on and around protestors to escape.

Arrests began sooner this time, five minutes after police cleaned up debris from the broken barriers. A third of the sit-down protestors retreated to the prayer warrior line to avoid arrest. We decided not to wait until the police had cleared away the protesters and instead smuggled clients into the clinic by putting an escort vest on them and slipping them through the side of the plywood wall.

The police seemed less patient this time. Many were working a double shift or on their day off and were tired. The weather was hot. Doing duty at an abortion clinic was a low priority for most of them, and the officers snapped more at the escorts. The chief was especially annoyed that we had smuggled in all the scheduled clients. This time over 150 arrests were made.

When the third attack of Operation Rescue came two months later, we were getting tired of dealing with people who obstructed the sidewalk. We decided not to put up any plywood wall this time, in hopes that the protestors might get a stiffer penalty for actually trespassing on private property. The previous arrests had resulted in charges of obstructing traffic.

This time the clinic's owner stood in front of the locked door to prevent protestors from gaining entrance. We had heard OR planned to bus in hundreds of people from other cities. That day's demonstration produced 175 arrests and twice that number of prayer warriors—a lot of people crowded on a city block. However, this effort gathered the least news coverage; each OR attack received less news coverage than the previous one.

This demonstration brought a Fort Wayne church to make a public pro-choice stand for the first time. The large Presbyterian church across from the clinic had a pastor who had escorted a few times. This church now arranged to have the clients wait inside in a private and comfortable parlor until arrests were over. I was thrilled to see several lay persons and the senior pastor wearing escort vests as this church reclaimed the old tradition of providing sanctuary or refuge to the oppressed.

When the arrests were finished, the escorts walked the clients directly past the prayer warriors, who began to mob them viciously, pressing on them and screaming. The police stood by and did nothing to stop the mobbing or to arrest those involved. After all the clients were inside the clinic, I told the clinic owner how much I admired the courage of the women who were willing to keep their appointments at the clinic in spite of all this harassment. The owner replied, "It shows you that a woman will go through anything to get an abortion."

The abortion battle in Fort Wayne gained international attention. In the fall, a camera crew from the British Broadcasting Corporation in London arrived to film a documentary, "The Debate," for *Everyman,* a British television series on social issues. Because abortion clinics in Europe are not picketed and no church groups there are trying to overturn abortion laws, the clinic situation in the U.S. is novel. I happened to be escorting during the day of filming; for the cameras, both the escorts and the protestors were on their good behavior. Nevertheless, the boyfriend of one client knocked down a BBC cameraperson; we tried to explain that the film would not be shown in the U.S. At one point the director asked us to shout more and be rowdy so she would get a more dramatic picture. I suppose the final product looked boisterous enough because several months later the clinic received a supportive letter from a Scottish woman observing, "It looks like hell over there."

In March, 1990 the volunteer escorts in Fort Wayne disbanded because of a federal court injunction. The clinic's owner, hearing that Operation Rescue was planning yet another attack, sued to have the protestors stopped. The clinic won the lawsuit. The judge's ruling forbade "rescues" and laid down strict guidelines on how the weekly protests were to be conducted. These guidelines prevented escorts from assisting patients, the judge reasoning that if the protestors were restricted, escorts would not be needed. Some escorts continued to come to the clinic on procedure days to carry pro-choice signs, but most appreciated the injunction because the continual anger was not healthy.

The escorting experience changed me. Previously uninformed and indifferent about the abortion issue, I became strongly pro-choice. I met other feminists and grew aware of other aspects of women's oppression. Now I pay more attention to other political issues. My faith now includes the awareness that many congregations need to have their consciousness raised on issues regarding women. Likewise, many feminist groups need to make efforts not to be so strongly anti-religious. Certainly safeguarding women's choices includes the choice of religion too.

17

Marching for
Women's Lives   §

Sally Carpenter

The prospect of ever achieving equality for women in
the United States seemed increasingly remote in the early '90s.
While Patricia Bowman, Anita Hill and Désirée Washington
shared publicly their experiences of rape and sexual harassment,
President George Bush reaffirmed the "gag rule" for clinics
(prohibiting even the mention of abortion during counseling of
women who tested positive for pregnancy in 4,000 federally
funded clinics). Operation Rescue targeted clinics in Wichita,
Kansas, and assaulted them for weeks. Meanwhile, the Catholic
bishops in the U.S. released a pastoral letter that upheld
women's equality while continuing to oppose both abortion and
women's ordination. The U.S. Senate included only two women
in its hundred members. Women in armed services could not
obtain abortions at military hospitals, while those same women
participated in a war to support Kuwait—a country that

oppresses women. Susan Faludi's book *Backlash* revealed how women's rights were losing ground. The Evangelical Lutheran Church in America adopted an anti-choice stance, while the Catholic and Southern Baptist leadership united to fight abortion. Guam, Louisiana, Pennsylvania and Utah passed highly restrictive abortion laws. The U.S. Supreme Court, packed with Reagan-Bush conservatives, heard arguments on Pennsylvania's abortion law, and many women feared that their decision would lead to even more restrictive laws. American women seemed to be on the brink of an age of repression.

To reactivate the pro-choice majority in the country, the National Organization for Women organized the second March for Women's Lives in Washington, DC, in April, 1992—modeled on other marches such as the 1989 march that brought out 300,000 people. From Fort Wayne alone some 150 chartered a bus or flew to the nation's capitol. After riding all night, those of us on the bus arrived early on a chilly Sunday morning, along with 300 other buses from all over the country. We parked at the Pentagon—where a parade volunteer asked us to sign an official march count sheet to help obtain an exact attendance count. Decked out with our many pro-choice buttons—including one I made saying, "Protestants Protest for Choice"—we gathered our signs and went to the march site. My sign said, "Methodist for Choice."

A subway ride to the Ellipse in front of the Washington Monument brought us to a pre-march rally. We didn't have time to sightsee, but I did see the simple, granite NOW monument on a small hill in the Ellipse—the only monument in Washington not dedicated to a man—which says, "Dedicated to the courageous women who died from unsafe, illegal abortions because they had no choice.'' Tears came to my eyes as I thought of the many lives the memorial represented.

The religious presence at the march was comparatively small—but noticeable. Catholics for a Free Choice (CFCC) put stickers on everyone who walked by. The Religious Coalition for Abortion Rights conducted a service in a small amphitheater and gave out posters in English, Spanish and Hebrew. I was glad to see women and men of faith present at the march because many people, especially those opposed to abortion, assume that all Christians oppose abortion.

When the rally began at noon, the crowds were so immense that the Fort Wayne group found itself too far away from the grandstand to see the speakers. However, the excellent sound system let us hear everything. Most of the speakers were pro-choice politicians running for office. But there were other luminaries including Geraldine Ferraro and Peter, Paul and Mary, who sang a pro-choice song written for the occasion.

Among the hundreds of posters being carried were some I would just as soon forget but others were memorable: ''I Asked God and She's Pro-Choice,'' ''Abortion, a Divine and Constitutional Right,'' ''Forced Pregnancy Increases Church Membership.'' My own sign led me into a number of conversations. A Unitarian pastor who had come with 60 members of her congregation congratulated me on my witness. I enjoyed meeting a United Methodist woman from DC whose church includes a founder of RCRC. During the entire march that day I saw only four anti-choice protestors, who stood quietly along the curb.

The march along Pennsylvania Avenue ended at the Mall beside the Capitol. By the time we reached the Mall, about three hours after the first marchers had left the Ellipse, estimates placed the crowd at anywhere from half to nearly a million people—the largest group to assemble in Washington in over two decades.

On the Capitol steps, in front of a reflecting pool, a grandstand held a seemingly endless stream of post-march speakers. Again our view was blocked by the hundreds of thousands of people around us. I was glad that two prominent church leaders were among those who spoke: Jesse Jackson, who revved up the crowd and then Ignacio Castuera, pastor of the Hollywood United Methodist Church in California, who pointed out that the timing of the march was close to several great religious festivals: Purim, when Esther saved the Jewish people from destruction; Passover, celebrated in song by Miriam; and Easter, when women were the first to witness Jesus' resurrection. Women, he stressed, have played critical roles in religion and women cannot be denied their humanity or dignity.

The speakers were still going strong when we had to leave to catch our bus back to Indiana. On the long ride back to Indiana, we were too tired to make much conversation and I actually went to work at eight as usual after arriving home at five a.m. Later in talking with friends about this experience, someone asked me if I thought marches were effective. This one certainly didn't seem to impress President Bush, who on the day after the march reaffirmed his anti-choice stance urging the U.S. Supreme Court to overturn the 1973 *Roe* v. *Wade* decision. Perhaps his defeat in the 1992 election shows how out of touch he had become with the those who were willing to demonstrate to the world their pro-choice stances. But marches are also just plain fun, motivating and inspiring the participants to continue the fight back home—if only this zeal carries on into less glamorous activist work once the buttons and banners are put away.

Two weeks after the march, Operation Rescue struck Buffalo, New York, to stage another Wichita-type siege. The pro-choice forces organized and kept the clinics open by forming human chains. By the end of the 13-day siege, 597 anti-abortion demonstrators had been arrested for trespassing, disorderly conduct and resisting arrest. These two events—the March for Women's Lives in DC and the OR harassment in Buffalo began and ended the month of April, 1992—two opposite points of view on the abortion issue. *The World Almanac and Book of Facts 1993* reported only the Buffalo event, however, under the title "Opponents of Abortion Lead Protest in Buffalo." Somehow the nearly one million marchers for a woman's right to choose were not as important as the 596 protestors arrested.

There was poor conduct on the part of both sides during the Buffalo siege, including an OR man who displayed the shriveled corpse of a stillborn baby and a clinic escort who spat on a Bible. Yet I was struck by the public statements of Randall Terry, founder of OR, that he hates feminists and that feminism leads to "disregard for authority"—male authority, no doubt. He once admitted that he grew up in a household of strong-minded women. Perhaps he is frightened by strong-minded women who do not rely on male guidance and make men like himself appear weak.

Terry's words, combined with the pastoral letter being circulated among Catholics, the imbalance of men in the Senate and so many other small pieces, suddenly seemed to fit together in a shocking picture. Surely the anti-choice movement has more to do with repressing the power of women than with protecting babies.

We are fortunate that since the 1992 march there has been a change of administration in Washington, which bodes many favorable changes for women—and not only for those needing abortions. Unfortunately, during this same period those who want to repress the power of women in the area of choice have grown more sinister—notably in the murder of Dr. David Gunn early in 1993. When extremists go as far as harassing pregnant women and shooting a doctor, we can see that the central issue is not a concern for life, but a struggle for power. Taking the life of a doctor because of a professed concern for unborn babies is outrageous. The real motivation is much deeper and rooted in the desire to control women.

Many Christians are reluctant to face the shocking fact that some church leaders as well as those in the congregation are using the Bible and the authority of the church to repress women. Surely this behavior is far from the life and words of Jesus Christ.

My prayer is that in the years to come Christians will be more visible in the pro-choice movement so that the myth that ''all Christians oppose abortion'' can be dispelled.

18

Church-Sanctioned Rape §

Mary Helen Spencer

While counseling a 15-year old rape victim and her parents recently, I realized that in nearly 25 years of pastoral counseling, none of the rape victims who had spoken with me had chosen to report the rape. I asked myself, "Why?" Upon reflection it occurred to me that those who had come to me for counsel and spiritual healing had been either victims of date-rape (about which I had read) or victims of institutionally sanctioned rape (of which I had seen absolutely nothing in print).

Since 1850 when Nathaniel Hawthorne published *The Scarlet Letter,* it has been acknowledged that elements of religious societies conspire to shield the male clergy from the necessity of accepting responsibility for their illicit sexual affairs, while the women involved bear the social and religious opprobrium. The problem, of course, is older than colonial America. In early Israel, Eli's sons, who were the hereditary ministers of the tabernacle, were punished by God for sacrilege because they raped and seduced the women who served at the sacrificial offerings (1 Sam 2:12-34).

Discerning the difference between rape and seduction in religious institutions today is difficult because of the young age of the girls involved and the amount of power the clergy wield within their own social and religious communities. Any attempt at such discernment in this context is rank hypocrisy since it is designed to determine the amount of guilt and responsibility to assign to the young women. Instead, we must recognize that the deliberate and planned seduction of very young women and very vulnerable women is rape. Apparently the Old Testament holds this view since God's judgment in this instance fell on the men and not the women—at a time in history when women were stoned for adultery. The record in Samuel is clear. God says, "And tell [Eli] that I am about to punish his house for ever, for the iniquity which he knew, because his sons were blaspheming God and he did not restrain them" (1 Sam 3:13). The leadership of a religious institution is responsible for violence done to women within its jurisdiction.

In the cases that have come to my attention, initially a 15- or 16-year-old girl is raped by the clergyman, his son, or the son of a leading layperson in the congregation. The girl is then pressured not to tell anyone and is subjected to mental and spiritual abuse ("You are a bad person. ... You can't be forgiven."). Then she is further sexually abused by the original rapist and other men or teenage boys in the group who have been informed by the rapist that the girl is available and will not inform on them. Even though rumors seep out among the congregation, no one investigates because of the power structures. Attitudes such as the following tend to prevail: "Boys will be boys," "She's that kind of girl," "She enjoys it," "It's just hanky-panky,'' and ''Let's not rock the boat.''

This kind of problem often occurs in a church that preaches strongly against abortion. If this girl gets pregnant, her parents are informed that she is the worst kind of sinner and that she must carry the baby to term as a punishment for her sins because ''human life is sacred.'' No one—least of all the religious professionals who are shielding this evil in their congregation—bothers to mention that the life of the defiled girl is also sacred and that Christians have a moral obligation to work together to help restore her life to her.

In this context, I believe it is a moral imperative to keep abortion safe and legal and available as a choice for such young women and their parents. It is well-known that there is greater medical risk for a young teenager to carry and bear a child than for a woman whose body is more mature. Under such circumstances there are many medical, psychological and social reasons why having an abortion may begin the healing process for a girl whose virginity, spiritual life and social acceptance have been taken from her by violence.

I have counseled with people from two different evangelical churches, one on the East coast and one in the West, in which the choir was being used to recruit young people for immoral purposes. (Both of these churches included young men as well as young women as targets of their evil practices.) In one case, when the senior pastor was made aware of the problem, he chose not to confront his staff members. It took several years for a huge public scandal to end the situation. The congregation was happy to get rid of the staff person who was central to the problem but refused to hold the senior pastor responsible for allowing the evil to continue. After all, he is a powerful, nationally known leader of whom the congregation is very proud.

In the other church, the pastor is deeply enmeshed in the problem. Since this church is independent, there is no denominational machinery higher than the local level with which to confront the pastor and his hand-picked staff and board. Consequently, this church continues its recruitment of young people through the choir for sexual exploitation. There is, however, a small but earnest group of people whose lives have been devastated by the evil in that congregation who are fervently praying for God's judgment on the hypocrisy in this church with its nation-wide reputation for being "Bible-believing."

In another conservative church that teaches women to be submissive to men, a male pastor who was responsible for a young woman becoming pregnant ordered his wife to invite the girl to stay in their home rather than go to a home for unwed mothers. Then he and his wife legally adopted the baby and raised it with their own three children. Although the congregation knew what was going on, instead of objecting, they announced that the pregnant girl was scum and that the wife who took her in was a saint. The pastor was touted as a "very fine minister who had made a mistake" but was "making restitution" by keeping the girl at his house and making his wife raise the child. One can only wonder if he had contriving sexual motives for keeping her in his house. Is it surprising that today this young woman professes atheism?

I know of another conservative religious group where a mentally unstable young woman was raped by one of the elders. When the congregation found out that she was pregnant, they called her their "little Magdalene" and adopted her baby into a church family. The elders told her parents that getting professional counseling would add to her sins and that the elders would be responsible for giving her the proper "Bible-centered" counseling she needed. Her family stayed in the church, and the daughter remained single because the elders never gave "Magdalenes" permission to marry.

Are these supposed solutions really morally superior to abortion? Or are they very sick ways of coping with human tragedy?

Only when their daughter became suicidal did one family discover a rape/seduction problem that had begun at summer camp and was continuing in the youth group. Another family could not understand why their daughter refused to go to church and hated Christians. In spite of her use of foul language when talking about the church group, the family remained unable to decode her suffering. She had been raped by several boys in her youth group and had been totally unable to cope because the situation was being protected by the institution. When she came to me, she said, "I couldn't tell the pastor because I was afraid he would do it to me, too." Three years later after professional counseling and prayer for healing of memories, she has begun to regain her spiritual equilibrium—but she cannot worship in a Christian context. Today she is studying Islam "because Moslems, in the name of God the Merciful and Compassionate, respect and protect their women."

These rapes are not reported because the psycho-social-spiritual trauma is overwhelming to girls in their early teens and the power is all on the side of the male perpetrators. Teenagers are deeply affected by peer pressure and the need to belong. Churches play on that need in order to gain new members. In the youth groups, church camps and choirs where rape and seduction are practiced, the modus operandi is based on the idea that "Our group has a secret from the religious fanatics in our church who want to spoil our fun."

After a girl has been raped—sexually initiated against her will—she is told that if she keeps quiet about it, she will remain an insider in the group, participating in its activities, which include becoming sexually active. Or she can tell—in which case they promise to ruin her reputation at church and school by portraying her as a slut and prostitute. At 14 or 15, a girl may believe, when given the choice between being an insider-slut or an outsider-slut, that she has no alternative. The trauma of the rape combined with peer pressure, institutional collusion and her own immaturity make it impossible for her to cope. This trap is especially confining for church children who are taught that if there is something they don't feel they can talk over with their parents, their only alternative is going to their pastor or youth leaders.

When teens, both boys and girls, know that the institution is turning a blind eye on illicit sex in its youth constituency, can we wonder why they choose to become sexually active and become accepted by their peer group?

In other cases a school is the institution protecting teenaged rapists. Several families have come to me for counseling from widely separated geographical locations where school authorities protected young boys who had committed rape. One high school girl was raped and beaten. When her father tried to talk with the guilty boy's father (a highly placed attorney), he was told, "Don't even think of going to court. The only lawyer in this county who would touch the case will prove your daughter is a whore and we will be sure that it gets in all the local newspapers.'' Discovering that other girls had also been victimized by this same male teenager, the father then turned to the principal of the public school, who replied, ''We know that this is going on, but what can we do when we are up against county power?''

In another state some junior high school boys were making plans to gang-rape a girl at an out-of-town honors student meeting where the students were to stay overnight at a hotel. One of the boys warned the girl, and her parents did not allow her to go on the trip. (Consequently, she forfeited the award she had earned for her honors paper.) The following week those same boys were shoving and kicking her, hitting her and calling her a whore on the school grounds. Her father went to talk to the principal, only to find that several adults were aware of what was happening and chose not to do anything about it because the girl was outspoken in her opinions and non-conformist in dress. ''If she would act a little more normal, they would quit bothering her'' was the message he received from the authorities at this public school.

I also counseled a missionary family who left their mission and took secular jobs in order to remove their daughter from a situation of sexual harassment and rape in a mission school.

In one of these three cases, the parents decided that abortion was the best decision they could make to help their daughter rebuild her life. Though the entire situation of rape condoned by school authorities is morally reprehensible, some people would apply that label only to the abortion decision.

Christian colleges are also part of this problem of institutionally sanctioned rape. I know of a half dozen small Christian colleges where the administrations refuse to acknowledge the violence against women occurring on the campuses. Consider the irony: they refuse to protect the daughters of parents who are paying astronomical fees to send their daughters to "a nice Christian college" in order to protect them from "the giant heathen state university."

The parents I know who have chosen to confront these colleges (from the level of deans up to the presidents) report various answers. At liberal schools, the answer is: "They are adult human beings. They can do as they please." The real meaning, given the dynamics of college pressures, is that the males can do as they please. At conservative schools, the parents are told, "Of course we don't have that sort of thing on this campus. Well, there may be a statistically small percentage of girls who are *that kind* and would be promiscuous no matter which college they attended." This evasion is tantamount to accusing the parents of having a daughter with loose morals.

Two of these Christian colleges that have turned their backs on rape/seduction victims are at this time facing bankruptcy. Though some Christians feel sad about their demise ("Such a fine institution," "a history of great service to the church," etc.). I disagree. These colleges were doing great disservice to God's work and needed to be closed. I would not give financial support to institutions that foster violence against women—only to those committed to biblical equality and justice.

Institutional sanctioning of rape occurs not only in individual churches and schools but at the denominational level. A female missionary from a church that sends many single women to the mission field shared her private ordeal with me. When she was experiencing burn-out from her work in the tropics, she was seduced by a clergyman who took advantage of her loneliness and mental fatigue. She admitted that humanly speaking, the situation was understandable though regrettable. What embittered her, however, was the psychological and spiritual blackmail that followed. The pastor who seduced her told other male clergy friends that they could go to her for "sex therapy." These others told her that they would report her earlier seduction to the mission board if she did not comply. After a long rest and professional counseling, she was strong enough to tell the blackmailers to "publish and be damned." She then left that mission organization and took a secular job, eventually finding peace with God through the sacrament of penance in the Roman Catholic church.

These are stories of people whose lives have been devastated by deliberate and entrenched evil. Deeply committed to their churches and communities, they have been betrayed and denied justice by institutions too large and powerful for them to stand against. These (and many others whose stories are not included) are individuals and families whom I have met personally and who have in various ways invited me into the healing process in their lives. Because I work at the national level of a large inter-denominational enterprise, I see people from all over the U.S. and from many denominational backgrounds. The incidents related here occurred within various groups along the whole spectrum of organized Christianity: from the Roman Catholic church through Presbyterian, Methodist and Baptist churches to Pentecostal churches and the Plymouth Brethren.

Christians must stand against evil within their institutions. Christian women must network, teaching girls to be alert for yet one more form of violence against women. Christian men must wake up to the kinds of evil that tend to be shielded by male bonding; they must be willing themselves to forfeit their own power within institutions for the sake of human justice and God's righteousness, and they must teach boys to be willing to do the same. Then Christian communities need to work together to provide a full range of healing options including both adoption and abortion for the families and individuals wounded by the evil in their midst.

The victim of violence must not be abandoned to face the struggle to rebuild a holy life. Courageous, mature leadership is required to lead congregations into repentance for the materialism, power politics and spiritual lethargy that allows wickedness to destroy human lives. People who come to the church to find new life in Christ need to be given bread, not stones.

For the woman who has experienced institutionally sanctioned rape, part of rebuilding her life may be a decision about a pregnancy. Some today are attempting to pass legislation that severely narrows or prohibits the availability of abortion. Such legislation is a gross injustice and reflects a grave misunderstanding of the ability of young women to cope with the trauma of rape. Unless the perpetrator is a stranger, young women usually do not report the rape. Societal judgments maintain that the girl is responsible for date-rape discourage victims from telling anyone. The sense of shame and failure at not standing up against the rape and seduction practiced within church groups also keeps people from getting help.

Until they are sure they have missed a menstrual period (which could be up to five weeks after the trauma), women are often in total denial and unable to deal directly with a rape situation. Even then, they may choose the path that lets them tell as few people as possible, going to a clinic for an abortion and attempting to rebuild their lives without any counseling or support. Many women have said to me, "I felt that I got myself into this, so I had to get myself out of it." Because of a girl's immaturity and lack of resources, "getting oneself out" may lead to bad decisions such as quitting school, moving in with some sympathetic fellow who takes further advantage of her, or making a hasty and unsuitable marriage.

In my ministry I have met many women who were unable to tell anyone of their rape and/or abortion for years after it happened. They may finally do so, however, either because of a further sexual trauma (which together with the original becomes unbearable) or because of an overwhelming experience of God's love and acceptance. Opening their hearts to a counselor, even years later, helps them to begin rebuilding their inner lives.

Self-acceptance, the first building block in a new life, is absolutely essential. Here we face the privacy issue and the Bill of Rights. Privacy is the bedrock on which self-acceptance can be built. Not to be able to accept oneself as a Christian or a decent member of society constitutes slow psychological suicide. Coping in private with a trusted friend or counselor is as much as many women can bear—without the added pressures from government, society and church community. Without privacy, a woman is vulnerable to hurtful messages spoken and implied.

The Supreme Court recognized the importance of a woman's privacy, guaranteed by the Bill of Rights, and made it the basis of the *Roe* v. *Wade* decision. Another example of the importance of privacy is demonstrated by the women contributing chapters to this book who chose to use pseudonyms to tell their stories, feeling a need to keep such personal and traumatic events out of public scrutiny. In cases where a group of people is involved, as with a school or church, clues about the identity of one person may give away the identities of others who may be having their own struggle to come to terms with the trauma and betrayal they have experienced.

God's grace surrounds each of us with love, acceptance, forgiveness, and new life for the whole person: spiritual, psychological, social, and physical. Christians are the bearers of that grace for one another. Within the family of God's love, all options that consider the needs of the whole person must be available. Arrogance and rigidity on both sides must be avoided. Some young women and their families are strong enough to opt for adoption or keeping the baby. Others may not be. In either case, God's grace is available to see us through a difficult and heart-breaking reality. Each person is promised, no matter what her pilgrimage may bring, that God will restore her life in Christ.

In Psalm 30 we read:

Thou hast not let my foes rejoice over me.
O Lord my God, I cried unto Thee for help,
    and Thou hast healed me....
Weeping may tarry for the night,
but joy cometh in the morning.''

Isaiah reminds us that "Mourning will be turned to dancing, beauty will be given for ashes'' (Is 61:3). We have these promises because God's mercies "never come to an end; they are new every morning; great is thy faithfulness'' (Lam 3:22-23).

19

Reflections—
On Morality §

Faith Annette Sand

A Michigan judge ... said he would grant permission for abortions only to white girls raped and impregnated by black men.... Judge Francis Bourisseau [said] he doesn't approve of abortion except in cases of rapes of whites by blacks and for victims of incest.... [When] asked ... about his comments on rape, Bourisseau said, "I just told it like it was." Then he hung up. —USA TODAY (International Edition), April 27, 1991

In musing on Judge Bourisseau's truth-telling, I reflected on my own heritage of resolute believers. Unlike the judge, my Minnesota relatives were not renowned for "telling it like it is" because there were some things you just did not talk about. Abortion would certainly have been a *verboten* subject. They did little wavering when it came to deciding virtuous behavior, even though a few skeletons peeked out of closets occasionally. But there was no white-washing, festooning, or pretending that the debauched were moral or that sexual sins were race-specific.

I wondered whether our French surnamed judge had been raised in a cultural world very different from my own. Sexual mores do tend to be culturally-specific. For example, when my parents embarked on a missionary career within weeks after my birth, they arrived in the then-unheard of Andean city of Medellín and learned that it had 4,000 registered prostitutes. Furthermore, these women were allowed to confess regularly in the Roman Catholic Church and thus be considered among the communicating faithful. As good Lutherans, my parents were incensed.

Three decades later I observed the same easy acceptance of the inadmissible when I was interviewing a renowned South American Catholic prelate who was trying to counter the surge of military violence in his country. He told me in confidence the details of how one prominent journalist—a supposed suicide—had actually been executed by the military. This information had come to him from one of his flock who happened also to be a prostitute and the favorite paramour of the military officer in charge, so I could not use the story in my report; he needed to guard his source of information. At least internally I arched an eyebrow.

When I projected how this anecdote would play among those I knew back in Minneapolis, I cringed. These were the days of easy, rigid lines between right and wrong. The family was God-fearing, upstanding and unadulterating. No prostitute in our circles would be told her sins were forgiven because of her economic plight, nor would my family excuse her behavior because of the influence of greedy capitalists on the economy of her city and country—I thought. Yet on one visit home I found myself with my aunts during the middle of the day waiting for them to finish watching their favorite soap opera.

My aunts discussed the plot with relish—an incredible round of adultery, divorce, betrayal, immorality and criminal behavior. It was a shocking juxtaposition to listen to these scoured and chaste women who always bannered principle, faith and duty to God discuss tales of the dregs of human behavior. I was appalled at how these upright Christian women could wallow in such muck with no qualms. They reminded me of the Latin prelate I had interviewed—personally chaste but trifling with the base.

My aunt's inexplicable viewing standards came into focus one day when abortion became the news item of the hour. As reporters discussed the violent attacks then going on at a Minneapolis women's health clinic, these women voiced their support for all the pressures being put on "those evil clinics that were murdering babies." They clucked a little at "the extremes" but did not condemn the tactics that to me appeared clearly monstrous. Just as in their soaps, they were ready to excuse a little rudeness from the anti-abortion foes, a little violation of someone else's rights, a little violence. In the end, they justified the attack and injury of the staff and clients of a clinic, calling it acceptable Christian behavior.

By this time in my mission career I had begun to question whether the abortion issue was not overblown. In my travels on church work, I had looked into the listless eyes of too many starving, emaciated babies and had shuddered at too many grimy, worm-bellied tots crawling in front of the squalor called home. Surely you could not call it murder to want to limit your family so that the children you did bring into the world had some prospect other than an early death. Along with birth control methods, should not abortion be available to a family unable to feed children already born? And the women victimized by rape, incest and abuse—should they not be able to decide whether the life they carried within them was to be brought to fruition?

I thought of Bourisseau and others who blink at racism yet scream about abortion. They want women whose birth control has failed to finish the pregnancy no matter what. Yet people with headaches, sprained toes, and contorted digestive tracts are not told to grin and bear it; our stores are filled with over-the-counter medicines to cure such aches and pains. Nor are those who suffer from cancer told that God wants the natural processes to go unhindered. Those who profit from the health care system make sure that a lot of unnatural, if not downright cruel, procedures are instituted—for a hefty fee—to keep the ravages of cancer at bay.

As I thought about these contradictions—dying children, excessive health care, and attacks on women's reproductive clinics—I concluded that my Christian family was forgetting part of their canon: "Judge not that ye be not judged." By strict pro-life standards, perhaps even God should be judged a murderer since some 50% of all conceptions abort spontaneously within the first trimester. To take a specific case, God condemned the innocent child born to David and Bathsheba to die as a consequence of David's sinful behavior toward Uriah. Was God unethical—or simply not as "pro-life" as today's extremists?

Another abortion issue that defies logic is the fact that no scientist can define precisely when human life begins or ends. This decision is culturally mandated. Anthropologists have observed a need within all cultures to maintain survival standards; without them, a tribe would die. Eskimos traditionally have gone out on ice floes to sleep their passage into the next world when the survival of the tribe is threatened by the care of a feeble and infirm member. In sub-Sahara Africa there are no-madic people who don't consider it a crime to expose a child before it starts to speak. Such children who would burden a tribe and threaten its existence are sacrificed with impunity. "Better that one member die than the whole tribe" has been decreed around the world for millennia. In my culture a living, pulsating heart is cut out of a body deemed "clinically dead" in order to pass the organ on to someone who could not continue to exist without it.

With so many of our ideas about the beginning and end of life culturally defined, who can dare make absolute statements about when life that is truly human begins? Experientially I know that the birth of my first child was an incredibly spiritual moment. With no advance warning, I suddenly felt surrounded by glorious angelic powers. Both of my children entered the world by natural childbirth, not because I chose this but because we were living deep in the jungles of Brazil where the benefits of electricity or other modern amenities were absent. Only kerosene lanterns were sputtering a few rays of light around that primitive delivery room. The doctor did not use any kind of drugs, so I was totally present and alert for that wonderful moment when the heavens opened. It made perfect sense to me! Of course, my baby's soul was being escorted into this bundle being placed in my arms. Intuitively I understood the lines, "... guardian angels round me keep." Ever after I have been in wonderful church services, meaningful religious retreats, quiet moments of prayer, but nothing was like that first glimmer of heaven's operations at

Heather's birth.

This experience also illuminated the Scriptures in a new way. As I reflected on Luke's story of the Christ's birth, it seemed obvious to me that the multitude of angels hailing the most-favored shepherds had just come off the grandest escort duty of all time! No wonder they wanted to shout about it. They showed up again at the other end of the Jesus's life, providing a round-trip escort service, it would seem. Rather than debate how many trimesters the creator of the universe spent *in utero,* I interpret the choir of angels as heralding the moment of incarnation.

As Christians we must not judge those who have found themselves in need of an abortion. No one knows when the unborn becomes a person. But we do know it is wrong for Judge Bourisseau to use his position to impose racially biased and immoral views on the world. Our model is Jesus, who showed mercy and grace in a situation where harsh judgment was being advocated. "Woman, where are your accusers?" Any other response is less than Christian.

20

Saying Yes to an
Unplanned Pregnancy   §

Anne Eggebroten

" "Our third child was a surprise," I sometimes admit in intimate conversations with other mothers. The phrase usually brings a knowing smile, or sometimes a woman responds by sharing a similar experience with a first, second or even a fifth child—occasionally ten or more years separated from the rest of the children in the family.

We are fortunate to live in a time when family planning is the norm, at least for middle-class families in the U.S. We expect to be able to control our fertility until we want children, and then we hope that the desired number of children will come on the schedule we have in mind. But having children is not that easy to plan. Sometimes, in spite of our best efforts, a pregnancy begins when we desperately don't want it to, or we find we cannot conceive a child in spite of the best efforts of medical science. When we cannot rationally and scientifically control our fertility, heartbreak is often the result. It is socially embarrassing when a couple cannot have a child or when a pregnancy begins at an unexpected time. The norm is *planning*.

I was fortunate enough to be able to control my fertility for nine years of marriage (two years on the pill and seven using the combined mucus/calendar/temperature method). Then we were blessed with two healthy daughters—a large enough family, we decided—so we began discussing birth control methods again, after having shelved the topic for five years. I wanted John to have a vasectomy, but he was fearful of medical side effects and the whole procedure. Convinced that I had done my fair share of birth control and birthing, I felt it was his turn to take responsibility in this area. To me, a vasectomy seemed like a minor, external annoyance compared to a woman's operation to get her Fallopian tubes tied. When he protested the pain of a vasectomy, I became eloquent on the physical suffering I had undergone in childbirth. After some months of argument, John agreed to take responsibility for our birth control—by using condoms. I agreed to this plan, relieved that he was taking a turn.

Eventually the night came when the condoms were not handy. We were on vacation and finding them might wake the children sleeping in the same room. My rough estimate of my previous calendar-keeping was that my fertile days were over; we took the chance. Two weeks later my period didn't come, and I began monitoring my temperature for the earliest sign of pregnancy—a rise in my basal body temperature. Within a week I knew I was pregnant again.

An unplanned pregnancy means a decision—and I am grateful the decision was in my hands, not that of the federal or state government. These circumstances were the impetus that produced this book, for I was suddenly forced to make a decision about an unplanned pregnancy. Many times I had said publicly, even in a formal debate setting, "I myself would never have an abortion, but I believe that abortion should remain legal." Throughout our early married years I knew that if our birth control failed, my husband and I would certainly keep the child. But now I had my heart set on returning to a teaching job and getting away from diapers; I wanted to spend at least a few hours a day with college students instead of toddlers.

Abortion had been a minor issue for me—the kind of thing I thought I should have a position on—yet my views kept changing. In 1970, just graduated from college, I asked my mother what she thought about abortion. She reminded me of what she had always told her four teenagers: "If you ever begin a pregnancy before you are married, I want the baby." But she also said that her experiences as a public health nurse in Colorado in the '50s had taught her that abortion should be available legally for use in some cases. "With judgment," she concluded. That phrase brought a smile to my face, for I knew she had used "judgment" many times over the years to justify a departure from the norm.

She gave me an example: a family who had five young children already, living in poverty in a small upstairs apartment with one set of grandparents—who happened to have tuberculosis. The T.B. had brought the family to her attention for they all had to be tested for the illness. The mother was pregnant again and desperate not to have another child. My mother asked a doctor she trusted if there was any way this woman could get an abortion, but he answered that no decent doctor would touch the case. The woman ended up completing the pregnancy and the circumstances of her life improved, but my mother was impressed with the fact that in some cases abortion did seem to be the most reasonable alternative.

In 1973, based on my mother's input, I felt rather positive when the *Roe* v. *Wade* decision made abortion legal in the first trimester and allowed state regulation in the second trimester. Because I had been married the year before, I thought abortion would remain an issue distant from my own life. Then in 1986, with a four-year-old and a two-year-old, I found myself wondering if a third pregnancy was "God's will for my life" or if God could understand my feelings of reluctance. I was 38 and it seemed ridiculous to be pregnant and starting over again on nursing and diapers—a phase in life I thought I had completed. I had planned to go back to work when my second child entered - school. Abortion surely wasn't an option for me—or was it? Married 14 years, financially secure, I certainly did not qualify as a desperate woman needing an abortion to make life livable.

Or did I? Staying home with two small children had shown me I was not cut out for spending all my waking hours with toddlers. I didn't have the patience or the ability to focus totally on them. I kept trying to squeeze in other things: part-time teaching, writing projects, or volunteer work. But trying to do these other projects with babies climbing on my lap, crying, or demanding "Look at me, Mama" while they invented dances and plays that could last for hours—it made for a life of built-in frustration. I ended up working on my own projects late at night when they were asleep—which often made me irritable and impatient the next day.

In my frustration I ended up screaming at them, throwing things or sobbing on my bed. My future stretched out bleakly:

John worked 12-hour days and I had no job possibilities on the horizon. Since I didn't feel good about putting children under two into child care, the circumstances of my life left me feeling trapped at home in a way I could not have imagined a decade before. As a dedicated scholar—a high school valedictorian with degrees from Stanford and Berkeley—I sometimes felt that my own life had ended when my children were born—the life of thinking, reading and talking with adults, maybe even going to a movie once in awhile. Now, just when I was hoping to get back to the kind of life I was more suited for, I faced another pregnancy.

Then I wondered if the baby would be normal. Our first two had been healthy babies, but at my age there was an increased possibility of carrying a Downs syndrome baby or one with some other serious deficiency. If I carried a child to the age when the amniocentesis is performed (which is also when the baby's kicks first start to be felt in the womb), I might not want to choose an abortion at that point even if it had a serious problem. Yet neither did I want to take on a lifetime job of caring for a disabled child.

John, knowing another child would affect my life more than his, was supportive of my concerns and willing to affirm whatever decision I came to. I prayed about what to do and came to feel that God also would be with me—whichever decision I made. It seemed as though God's will for me was not spelled out specifically as ''Complete this pregnancy'' or ''End it,'' but instead as ''This is what Yahweh asks of you: to act justly, to love tenderly and to walk humbly with your God'' (Mi 6:8). So it was, in complete freedom, not forced by my husband, my church or my government, I chose to have that baby. The experience of choosing was difficult but exhilarating. For a while I experienced some ambivalence about my decision, but I knew that at least it was my choice.

Three months later, when the amniocentesis told me that we were to have a girl, the miracle of bonding took place. I also saw my baby on the sonogram screen, and she became real to me. I wrote a poem to her, loving her and happy about her coming into my world. But one huge fact had changed my life: I had made a choice. During the rest of that pregnancy, I wondered what my life would have been like if I had not been able to choose this baby. How would I have felt if the federal government had told me that I *had* to have this baby? If I had not had the option of abortion, would I still be resenting this pregnancy? I knew the answer was yes.

What happens to a child who remains unwanted—at birth and even into childhood? As a child grows from diapers to the terrible twos to the teen years, there are many times when a parent's faith and patience wear thin. During those hard times, one relies on the underlying fact of commitment: *she is mine—I want this child*. What a different life that child would have without that parental commitment—what a dangerous situation if instead the mother still bore an underlying resentment about having to bear and care for that child. Statistics on child abuse took on a new meaning as I pondered the effects of forced child-bearing.

Suddenly the importance of keeping abortion safe and legal became clear to me. I had personal experience of the impact on me and my child if I were forced to complete a pregnancy. Having a choice is important for the woman who decides on an abortion, but it is equally important for the woman who decides to complete an unplanned pregnancy. Being forced to become a mother is a terrible thing. Love cannot be forced.

With this realization, I made a promise to myself and to God: yes, I would complete this pregnancy, but I would also collect stories to form a pro-choice book. Over the last seven years, however, one thing stands out among the many things I have learned: never start a book and a baby at the same time. One of them will not get much attention, and since babies can cry and laugh and coo, it will not be the baby that gets put on a back shelf.

Part 3

The Bible & Choice §

21

The Bible and Choice §

Anne Eggebroten

Should abortion be legal? Or should it be returned to the illegal status it had for about a century prior to 1973?

No matter who we are, our answer to this question will depend on our answer to two other questions:

- How serious an act is an abortion?
- How much do I respect someone else's view of abortion?

If we consider abortion to be as serious as murder, we may choose the most drastic means to prevent it—that is, we may ask the federal government to make abortion illegal again. If we consider abortion to be a minor office procedure to extract cells that would become a human, we may wonder what all the fuss is about. Many Christians, however, have adopted various positions on abortion in between these two extremes.

For example, some consider abortion to be a sad expedient, taxing to the woman both physically and emotionally, but not the equivalent of taking a life. These Christians prefer various less drastic means of preventing abortion. They choose to work through improved birth control, slow changes in our culture and media, increased support for women with unplanned pregnancies, and greater responsibility for men in handling their sexuality. Other Christians who themselves regard abortion as murder nevertheless respect divergent views and therefore choose to work through persuasion and education rather than through laws and the judicial system. Only those who do not respect the views of others try to implement laws forcing everyone to abide by their views.

As Christians considering these issues, we will turn to the Bible, or consult church doctrine, or discuss the matter with church leaders, or bring the question directly to God in prayer.

The Bible gives no clear answer regarding the seriousness of the abortion issue. It never actually mentions abortion and only twice mentions miscarriage.[1] We cannot find in the Bible an explicit statement on whether abortion is or is not "murder." Nevertheless, the Bible gives us guidelines about the value of human life, including the value in God's eyes of the life *in utero* that has the potential of becoming a full human being.

Regarding the second question—how much should we respect others' choices—the Bible is clear. We are not to force on others, particularly non-Christians, beliefs they do not understand or accept. We are to work by example, explanation, sup-

---

[1] D. Gareth Jones, *Brave New People: Ethical Issues at the Commencement of Life* (London: Inter-Varsity Press, 1984; rpt. Grand Rapids, MI: Eerdmans, 1985) 173. See also Kristin Luker, *Abortion and the Politics of Motherhood* (Berkeley: Univ. of Calif. Press, 1984). The two mentions of miscarriage in the Bible can be found in Exodus 21:22-24 and Exodus 23:26. The first describes a miscarriage due to injury and the fine to be paid by the person who caused the injury. The second promises that those who serve God will not miscarry (a part of the covenant code).

port and prayer to persuade others to abide by the highest values, but we are not to force these on others.

When we debate the abortion issue, we may discover that words and arguments do not go far. Most of us form our values and beliefs not through rational analysis but through grappling with our experiences. We love God because we have experienced God's love for us, not because we have come to an intellectual conclusion that God exists and deserves our love.

The Eternal One communicates with us not just by a set of rules but by recording for us in the Bible the experiences of a chosen people interacting with God and with each other. When we read the Bible, our own experiences mold our perceptions and affect our views of David, Mary Magdalene, Paul and Phoebe. Likewise, our gender, our age, our marital status, our cultural background, and our unique journey all influence our view of the seriousness of abortion and of how we should go about reducing the number of abortions.

One way to overcome our limited background and get a larger view of the abortion issue and God's guidance on it is by listening to the experiences of others. The Christian women whose stories are recorded here have dealt with abortion at a personal level; they have faced it with dismay as an unexpected option in their lives. In unique, difficult circumstances each woman chose an abortion as the least injurious of the various unpleasant alternatives facing her. The personal stories in this book speak for themselves—from the young woman raped by her brother-in-law to the older woman for whom a third child would jeopardize her family's precarious stability.

After pondering these women's experiences, many Christians will come back to the question of whether there can be a theological, biblical basis for keeping abortion available legally. Perhaps we would like to respect the view of a woman in crisis that abortion is not seriously wrong and that it is a better choice than some of the other alternatives facing her—even if we disagree with her. Therefore we seek guidance from the Bible on this issue of abortion and whether it is serious enough to require others to live by our understanding of it.

To consider this question adequately, we must look not just at abortion but at the larger issue of procreative choice. Rosalind Pollack Petchesky draws us to this larger issue in her book *Abortion and Woman's Choice: The State, Sexuality, and Reproductive Freedom*.[2] For Petchesky, the fundamental decision is whether women will be allowed to bear children by choice. This is a new issue. A century ago, it was not possible for each pregnancy to be begun and completed by choice. Birth control and abortion were attempted, but often unsuccessfully. Unwanted babies were expected in women's lives. Today, however, birth control is more advanced, and when birth control fails, pregnancy can be detected and ended earlier. In fact, 51% of all abortions are done in the first six weeks after conception, when the embryo is less than one-half inch long. 91% are performed in the first ten weeks.[3]

Unfortunately as women have gained control over their fertility, elements in both the state and the church have been reluctant to see that control develop. Society, of course, has an interest in maintaining the supply of babies, and there is some fear over

---

[2] Boston: Northeastern Univ. Press, 1984.

[3] *Point Counterpoint* (Washington, DC: Religious Coalition for Abortion Rights, 1984) 14-15.

whether women, given complete procreative choice, will continue to bear children. Thus both the church and the state have an interest in retaining some control over reproductive decisions.

The Bible, however, does not support either church or state control over procreation. It places full responsibility for procreative choice in the hands of the parents. By the term *procreative choice* we mean *the full range of conditions necessary to insure that a couple will have a child only when they decide to do so.* This means that coercion will not be a part of child-bearing.[4] The decision to have a child must include the consent of both members of the couple—the man not forcing the woman into child-bearing, and the woman not forcing the man—unless she wants to take full responsibility for the child.

The conditions needed to insure procreative choice include:

- Less emphasis on and distortion of sex in the media and culture to which our children are exposed;
- Safe, 100% effective birth control methods;
- Men taking their share of responsibility for birth control;
- Men not forcing women into intercourse or into omitting birth control (either in marriage or outside);
- Men taking their share of responsibility for their children in everything from child care to financial support; and
- Women having an option for abortion when one or more of these earlier conditions has not been met and an unwanted pregnancy occurs.

Ideally procreative choice means both the father and the mother want the child. Should the two disagree on this decision,

---

[4]   Adapted from Beverly Wildung Harrison, *Our Right To Choose: Toward a New Ethic of Abortion* (Boston: Beacon Press, 1983), Chs. 1 & 2.

the woman's choice must take precedence. If only the woman wants to complete the pregnancy, at least one parent is committed to the life and care of that child. No man should force an abortion on a woman or demand she bear a child. The pain involved in her pregnancy and childbirth experience takes precedence over his potential loss in not having that child. Thus choice—not coercion—must govern child-bearing.

With this understanding of procreative choice, let us reflect on the Scriptures. A careful reading of the Bible reveals important themes that will lead us to support full procreative choice, as opposed to government involvement or coercion in child-bearing decisions. As anti-abortion activists are quick to point out, the Bible contains a strong emphasis on the value of human life. But there are other biblical precepts such as the greatest commandment (to love God and your neighbor as yourself) that must be weighed along with the affirmation of physical life.[5]

Five of the major areas that contribute support to full procreative choice are:

- covenant theology,
- crucifixion/rebirth theology,
- the doctrine of free will,
- the doctrine of salvation by grace, and
- the biblical vision of the kingdom of God.

In addition, the Bible gives us some clear guidelines about how to witness for our faith in a fallen world: to speak with gentleness, to work in servanthood, and to persevere in prayer. These guidelines, if heeded, would lead us to a position in favor of full

---

[5]   Mark Olson, "The Sanctity of Life: From Heresy to Hope," *The Other Side*, 23.6 (1987): 2.

procreative choice. The Bible gives us not only major theological themes reflecting on choice, but also practical guidelines.

The Value of Human Life

The most obvious biblical principle regarding procreation is the value of human life. There are so many passages that affirm this value—from John 3:16, "For God so loved the world that God gave God's only incarnate Self, that whoever believes in Jesus should not perish but have eternal life" to Psalm 139:1, 13, "O Lord, you have searched me and known me! ... You knitted me together in my mother's womb."

What the Bible says to us, and what we affirm to a needy world, is summed up in the first of the four spiritual laws described in Campus Crusade witnessing materials: "God loves you and has a wonderful plan for your life."[6] Jesus tried to give us an idea of the immensity of God's love and intimate knowledge of us by saying that God knows the number of hairs on our heads. The Psalmist sought to describe God's love and intimate knowledge of us by saying that even in the womb, "Thy eyes beheld my unformed substance" (Ps 139:16). The Creator not only knows us but had foreknowledge of us.

Some Christians move from God's foreknowledge of us in the womb to the sanctity and inviolability of the embryo or fetus, concluding that even the fertilized egg is a full person. Thus terminating the pregnancy, even in its earliest stages, is considered murder. These conclusions are understandable, but other Christians affirm the value of beginning forms of human life

---

[6] *The Four Spiritual Laws* (Colorado Springs: Navpress, 1962) p. 3.

without ascribing full personhood to them. They realize the seriousness of ending that potential life but refuse to call that termination "murder." The difference of opinion arises because the Bible is not explicit about the line between a person and a potential person.

In the absence of biblical clarification, we are left with the general principle of the value of human life. Some of us conclude that a life once begun is inviolable; others reach an opposite opinion and believe the most responsible decision in a given situation might be to end that developing life. Furthermore, the person who is actually facing the complex problem of what to do about an unplanned pregnancy will see it differently from someone merely considering it theoretically.

Whatever our view, we must all face the reality that two Christians studying the same Bible can come to different conclusions on this issue. In addition, non-Christians also debate the beginnings of life and the advisability of abortion, arriving at varied opinions. Does it thus make sense to advocate a law establishing the full personhood and inviolable rights of the developing embryo/fetus from the moment of conception? Is a law the best way to teach the world about God's love for each of us and about the preciousness of human life?

We need to emphasize the sacredness of life in our society, but trying to establish laws and punishments in this area is likely to set up a negative reaction that will actually inhibit learning about the sanctity of human life. The Bible presents the high value of human life, but an environment of freedom will teach that value better than an environment of coercion.

Covenant Theology

Another biblical principle that will guide us toward procreative choice is God's covenant relationship with us. From the first covenant with Noah and "all flesh that is upon the earth" (Gen 9:17) to the covenants with Abraham and Moses and the new covenant in the Christ, the Bible tells us that God is not just a remote creator who set the universe and the human race in motion. Rather God continues to be intimately involved with us and desires a covenant relationship that will guide us in wisdom and in glorifying our Maker.

Furthermore, Genesis tells us that we are created in God's image and that part of that image is to bear responsibility, "dominion ... over every living thing that moves upon the earth" (1:27-28). Certainly this charge includes responsibility for the children we create. Just as God creates us and then reaches out to us with the offer of a covenant, "I will take you for my people, and I will be your God" (Ex 6:7), we are to reflect God's image and conceive children only in the context of a covenant that says, "I have chosen you; I will love you, provide for you and guide you as you grow up." If neither the father nor the mother is willing to make that commitment, nor to trust surrogate parents to make that commitment, no one should force the woman to continue the creation process. No state or federal law should require more than one million children per year to come into this world in the U.S. alone without that kind of covenant from their parents.

Beverly Wildung Harrison, professor of Christian ethics at Union Theological Seminary in New York, develops this theme of a covenant theology in her book, *Our Right To Choose:*

Toward a New Ethic of Abortion. She concludes that people can no longer "bear children frivolously, in the absence of an act of radical love, one that says, 'I chose you, I welcome you, I covenant to be with you through the long and not always easy passage into life, and through your growth into a wider community of relation.' "[7] We need to respect human life enough to be careful about when we start it, to plan ahead and act responsibly. If this care and planning does not happen, if a couple has accidentally begun a life for which neither partner can make a covenant of love and caring, then there should be access to a safe, legal means of ending the pregnancy. The covenant basis of Judeo-Christian theology directs us toward bearing children only as part of a covenant, and that promise of commitment can be freely made only in the context of full procreative choice.

Crucifixion/Rebirth Theology

Another biblical paradigm that informs our decisions about bringing children into this world is our theology of rebirth. We believe that Jesus' death gave us the opportunity for spiritual birth into new life. Jesus even compared the crucifixion experience to the suffering of a woman in childbirth. During the Last Supper, when his disciples were confused and anxious about his predictions of his own death, Jesus reassured them by saying, "When a woman is in travail she has sorrow, because her hour has come; but when she is delivered of the child, she no longer remembers her anguish, for joy that a child is born into the world. So you have sorrow now, but I will see you again" (Jn

---

7   loc cit, pp. 116-117.

16:21-22). With this illustration, Jesus shows us that he has a high view of pregnancy and birth. He considers bringing a human life into the world to be a great sacrifice, like his own suffering on the cross to give us second birth and like the suffering of his friends as they see him dying.

Both kinds of life-giving sacrifice—women giving birth and Jesus giving eternal life—need to be done out of free will. To require a woman to complete a pregnancy against her will, dishonors her sacrifice. Her suffering is no longer freely chosen for a joyful purpose. It becomes coercion—a punishment for a mistake. The chief priests and Pharisees intended Jesus' death to be a punishment, but the foundation of all our theology is that Jesus *freely* chose to "submit unto death." If we eliminate the element of choice—if Jesus had been forced to the cross or if a woman is forced into child-bearing—the event becomes terrible and sad, not a joyous sacrifice in order to bring forth new life.

At first glance, the anti-abortion position seems to support motherhood, for it would create a million additional mothers annually in the U.S. alone—a tacit statement that motherhood is good. But by forcing motherhood on women who are not freely choosing it, an anti-abortion law would cheapen our view of pregnancy and motherhood. Instead of a holy and life-giving sacrifice freely chosen—like Jesus' sacrifice—pregnancy, birth, and motherhood would become for many a dreary punishment. Thus the quality of mothering would go down. Only when motherhood is freely chosen can its difficult work be valued—by the individual and society. If it is an involuntary side-effect of sexual intercourse, its value decreases for the individual and for society.

The Bible does not foresee a world in which full procreative choice is possible, but it does give us a theology centered on spiritual birth through the freely chosen sacrifice of Jesus on the cross. This theology requires the highest respect for women bringing life into the world—including respect for their own judgment about when and whether to make this sacrifice. As Harrison says, "Women as a group must be considered competent moral agents."[8] If our society does not grant individual couples full procreative choice—and if within the couple, the woman does not have complete freedom to choose—then we will have a world of forced, devalued motherhood and lack of respect for women. In a world in which choice is possible, the Bible gives no support to forced motherhood.

The Doctrine of Free Will

Another major area of Christian theology that favors procreative choice is the doctrine of free will with its emphasis on human responsibility. In his letter to the Romans, the apostle Paul affirms the importance of free will while struggling with the terrible responsibility it places on us all. Paul sees all humans as responsible before God for their choices, both good and evil: "There will be tribulation and distress for every human being who does evil, the Jew first and also the Greek, but glory and honor and peace for every one who does good, the Jew first and also the Greek" (2:9-10).

An important aspect of our being created in God's image is our ability to choose between good and evil. God does not govern our moral decisions. The Creator feels comfortable with letting us make our own choices and making us eternally respon-

---

[8]   Harrison, 16.

sible for those choices. Constantly we are faced with making moral choices, for better or for worse. Jesus certainly didn't make people's decisions for them, even in critical situations—in his interactions with John the Baptist, with Peter (even in his denial), with the rich young ruler, with the woman caught in adultery, with her accusers, with Judas in his betrayal and with Pilate in his decision to allow the crucifixion.

Thus both the Sovereign One in heaven and Jesus on earth demonstrated a willingness to live with the consequences of human wrong choices—in order for humans to have free will. Apparently the Creator sees a value in our making mistakes and bearing responsibility for our choices. God's ultimate purpose, of course, was to create a context in which humans could take part in the incredible beauty of the free choice to love and serve the Creator, following the One who became incarnate.

Unfortunately, we humans find it difficult to be this gracious with others. Frequently we resist allowing others to bear the consequences of their free will. We like control. Letting a woman making a difficult moral decision (regarding a potential human being within her) makes us nervous. We want a law to control her, to make sure that she makes the "right" decision. But Jesus says to us, "No ... judge not. Let *her* be responsible before me." If we work to pass an anti-abortion law, we would deny women whose birth control has failed the opportunity to weigh good and evil and to make a responsible moral decision— one that will affect them for the rest of their lives. We would instead place this decision in the hands of the federal or state government.

Yet if we look at the history of decisions made by our government—locally and nationally—we see mistakes as well as successes. Presidents, members of Congress, and other leaders have made life-or-death decisions that resulted in thousands of deaths. Some of these decisions—such as the bombing of Hiroshima and Nagasaki—are justified by many Americans, even if many deaths occurred. Others decisions were clearly mistakes. In 1988 a U.S. Navy officer in the Persian Gulf fired a missile at a civilian airliner, killing 290 people, including 66 children.[9] Somehow we can tolerate our leaders making life-or-death decisions affecting many lives when they are faced with difficult situations such as international aggression. We find understanding and empathy for them if they make a mistake—even if their decision brings death to other human beings, yet we don't want to let a woman make a decision affecting only her own life and the life within her.

If we respected women as a group, we would want to protect the laws and Supreme Court decisions that permit women to make complex moral decisions revolving around their choice to give birth. We would understand how a woman, faced with a difficult situation, must decide how to handle it to the best of her ability—even if that decision means ending a human life in its beginning stages within her. If we believed in the importance of free will as much as God does, we would not want laws eliminating women's choice in this situation. We would see that claiming "abortion is wrong no matter what" requires the average woman to adhere to a morality far more demanding than that which we require of our national leaders. We allow them to make hard life-and-death choices, but some of us want to hold a woman with an unplanned pregnancy to a single standard, no

---

9   John Barry and Roger Charles, "Sea of Lies," *Newsweek* 13 Jul 92:28-39.

matter the consequences for the baby or others involved.

To do so is to ignore the implications of the biblical doctrine of free will, which would guide us to give this woman procreative choice. As Christians, we could go further and her not only legal choice but economic and emotional support that might perhaps enable her to choose to complete the pregnancy, just as we might try to persuade world leaders to choose peace instead of a violent solution to their differences. But because of our belief in free will, we would limit ourselves to persuasion rather than employing legal force.

The Doctrine of Salvation by Grace

Another biblical theme that leads us to full procreative choice is the overarching presence of God's grace in each moment of our lives. For people who have put their faith in Jesus Christ as sovereign and savior, nothing can separate us from the love of God. In our culture, however, mistakes in the area of sexuality are often judged more harshly than others. Self-righteous Christians sometimes participate in this heavy judgment, but the Bible says, "There is no distinction; since all have sinned and fall short of the glory of God, they are justified by God's grace as a gift, through the redemption which is in Christ Jesus" (Rom 3:23-24). Salvation by grace, not by works, is the heart of Christian theology.

What is the best way to demonstrate God's grace to a pregnant, unmarried teenager? One young woman whose story is in this book was sent off to a home for unwed mothers to preserve the family's reputation. Another was forced to have an abortion to preserve the reputation of the young man—a prominent pastor's son. Her story could not be included in the book, even anonymously. Another young woman's father banished her, sold the house, and moved the rest of his family away to prevent them from being contaminated by her sin (see ch. 3). The pregnancy of another young woman (not in the book) was announced to the whole community and she was required to attend church where others ostracized and shamed her.

If we really took our theology seriously and believed in God's grace, we would not regard pregnancy out of wedlock as a sin to be censured above all others or to be covered up at any cost, even when it means untold cruelty toward women. We would help young women keep their babies or choose abortion, in either case supporting them with reassurance of God's continuing love for them. We would understand that in a fallen world— where sexual experimentation is rampant, where men are persuasive and don't expect to bear the consequences of their sexual actions, where institutional power protects the powerful—young women must have the recourse to safe, legal abortion.

Jesus' compassion and grace toward these young women can be seen in the story told in John's gospel, chapter eight. The scribes, the Pharisees, and the law of Moses were all lined up against the woman caught in adultery, and to most people the answer was clear: stone her. When Jesus came on the scene, he entirely changed the dynamics of the occasion and left us with a poignant story that teaches us that God's grace is more powerful than any human mistake. All have sinned, yet grace abounds. All human choices can be swept up into the redeeming current of the water of life. "Whoever drinks of the water that I shall give her will never thirst; the water that I shall give her will become in her a spring of water welling up to eternal life" (Jn 4:14).

Imagine for a moment that the woman caught in adultery

became pregnant, captured not only by the scribes and Pharisees but by her own biology. Rescued once from stoning, she misses her period and realizes that a pregnancy will soon expose her again to shame and possible death. She finds Jesus and falls at his feet, crying, "Help me!" Or perhaps she only touches his robe in a crowded street, praying to be healed from the sudden absence of her regular flow of blood.

> *And immediately her flow of blood began. And Jesus said, "Who was it that touched me?" ... And when the woman saw that she was not hidden, she came trembling, and falling down before him declared in the presence of all the people why she had touched him, and how she had immediately been healed. And he said to her, "Daughter, your faith has made you well; go in peace" (Lk 8:44-48).*

For women our flow of blood makes so much difference, whether it continues and cannot be stopped or whether it stops suddenly as a sign of pregnancy. Usually the news of beginning pregnancy is a time of celebration, but when it is not, a safe and legal way of ending the pregnancy should be available. Jesus can speak to the zygote or even fertilized egg, bless it, and call it back to God's presence. Perhaps he did this for the woman caught in adultery. Or perhaps he found for her a safe place to live while pregnant and a means of support for her and her child. This part of the story is not recorded, so we will never know. But if we make any decisions regarding women and adultery or pregnancy, let us err on the side of grace.

The Vision of the Kingdom of God

Another Christian belief that guides us toward procreative

choice is our faith in the coming sovereignty of God on earth. We want to "bring in the kingdom" as much as possible in our society. Returning from 40 days of testing in the desert, Jesus entered a synagogue and made his first announcement of God's imminent presence on earth, reading from Isaiah: "The Spirit of the Lord is upon me, because God has anointed me to proclaim release to the captives and recovering of sight to the blind, to set at liberty those who are oppressed, to proclaim the acceptable year of the Lord" (Lk 4:18-19).

Though ultimately referring to all of humanity, Jesus expressed specific concern for the poor, for captives, for those with a physical handicap, for those who are oppressed. As followers of Jesus, we are likewise charged to bring the good news of the realm of God to people in these categories and to assist them in their problems. When we encounter a poor woman with an unwanted pregnancy, we certainly must try to help her. She simultaneously lives within all four categories: she is poor and concerned about whether she can support another child; her body is captive and controlled for nine months by another life growing within her; she is handicapped by loss of mobility during her pregnancy; and she has probably been oppressed by the father who would not share in the responsibility for birth control or for the conceived child. She has also been oppressed by lack of access to cheap, safe, effective birth control methods. If we care about God's kingdom and justice, will we establish a law that further oppresses her by telling her that she cannot end her pregnancy?

If abortion is made illegal in this country again, the weight of the law will fall only on poor women. Those with access to economic resources will continue to have full procreative choice.

They will simply pay to see the right doctor or travel to another country. Only the poor will bear children they do not want or cannot adequately care for. Those who are desperate enough will attempt self-abortions or become victims of back-alley abortions.

The maternal mortality rate during pregnancy dropped dramatically in the U.S. in the 20th century as contraceptives became increasingly available. In one survey of 15 states in 1927-28, 794 women died from self-induced abortions (10% of the 7,537 pregnancy-related deaths).[10] In 1940, 1,682 women died from abortion in the U.S. (according to published reports—there were probably others for whom the cause of death was concealed). In the '60s, when abortion restrictions were easing, between 100 and 300 women died yearly from abortion complications in the U.S.[11] By 1979 (six years after *Roe* v. *Wade*) the number of women dying per year from abortion was less than one for every 100,000 live births.[12] If we make abortion illegal again, we will return to seeing 100 to 300 poor women or more die each year in botched abortions, not to mention those who will have serious complications but do not die. The U.S. would return to the tragedy of the developing nations where an estimated 200,000 women still die each year from unsanitary, illegal abortions. The International Fund for Family Planning estimates that 500,000 women die each year from childbirth related causes, and about half of these deaths could be prevented if women who want family planning services had access to them.

A kingdom theology demands that we work for the coming of

---

[10] Luker, 49, 74.
[11] Louise B. Tyrer, "Abortion in the U.S.: Past, Present, and Future?" *Issues in Reproductive Health* (New York: Planned Parenthood, 1982) 3-4.
[12] Luker, 283-284.

God's Dominion, and this work includes caring about the poor and about justice. If we cared about poor women, we would make a society where they had the economic resources to provide for all the children they wanted to bear—but until we get to such an ideal world, we must not require them to bear children for whom they have no economic resources. Reproductive freedom in a just society would give all women full procreative choice: the opportunity to enjoy children as well as the ability to prevent the birth of children they cannot enjoy.

Thus we have seen that five major areas of Christian faith—covenant theology, crucifixion/rebirth theology, the doctrine of free will, the doctrine of salvation by grace, and the vision of the kingdom of God—all support individual procreative choice as opposed to church or state control of procreation.

Guidelines to Witnessing

In addition, the Bible provides us with guidelines on how to witness to our faith in Jesus, God's chosen one, sent to redeem a fallen world. The Scriptures instruct us to:

- speak with gentleness,
- work in servanthood, and
- persevere in prayer.

Speak with Gentleness

This principle is expressed throughout Scripture. Peter puts it succinctly: "Always be prepared to make a defense to any one who calls you to account for the hope that is in you, yet do it with gentleness and reverence" (1 P 3:15). We are to live redeemed lives and to be ready to suffer for righteousness' sake.

Then, when others are attracted to "the hope that is in us," we are to introduce them to Jesus of Nazareth and a life that reflects a relationship with God. But certainly we are not to force the unconverted to behave according to our standards.

Some areas of morality, such as prohibitions against murder, historically have been part of all cultures. Other mores vary from culture to culture and age to age. For centuries, ending pregnancies before "quickening" was considered acceptable in Western cultures.[13] Now a number of organizations are advocating a ban on abortions from the earliest moment of conception. Respect for human life at all stages is certainly an admirable position, but the Bible cautions us against forcing our insights on those who are unconvinced.

When we encounter people with a grim, desperate outlook on life, we want to reach out to them as Christians. We would like these people to understand how beautiful, meaningful and valuable life can be. Suppose we find a young woman and her boyfriend who have such a view of life and also have an unwanted pregnancy. Our goal would be to communicate God's love for each of them, as well as for the beginning human life developing within the young woman. If we wanted to witness with gentleness, as Peter's letter advises, we would begin with a concrete demonstration of our concern for them, perhaps also showing them Bible passages about God's love for them. But what kind of a witness would it be if we simply quoted a law saying, "No matter what your beliefs are, you have to complete this preg-

---

[13] Jane Hurst, *The History of Abortion in the Catholic Church: The Untold Story* (Washington, DC: Catholics for Free Choice, 1981). See also Luker, chs. 2 & 3.

nancy. *We* believe in the sanctity of human life, so you'd better abide by it." Would this law convert them or teach them the value of human life? (Or would it just make them even more bitter against the Christians who passed this law?) To make two people's lives even more desperate and difficult, when they already have a cynical view of life, is not the kind of Christian witness advised in the Bible.

Suppose instead we encounter a responsible atheist with a family—a person who does not believe in eternal life or that the fertilized egg has a soul or is a person. How will this person react if conservative Christians succeed in establishing a law that reflects a religious belief in the sanctity of human life from the moment of conception onward? Such a law could make non-Christians angry and hinder our primary task of sharing the gospel with others. After all, 58% of all Americans believe a woman has a Constitutional right to an abortion in the first three months of her pregnancy, according to a Gallup poll in 1989.[14] The Bible tells us our goal should be to change minds and hearts, not to change the law on a controversial and personal issue.

Work in Servanthood

The Bible also calls us to servanthood and humility as the Christ-like means of approaching any problem. When the disciples began arguing over "which of them was to be regarded as the greatest," Jesus explained that unlike secular authority which exercises "lordship," he chose to come "among you as one who

---

14 "Wrestling With a Painful Issue" *Newsweek* 17 July 1989: 15.

serves'' (Lk 22:25-27). He contrasted two possible methods of influence: the use of authority vs. servanthood.

The Christ-like way of reducing the number of abortions is through servanthood—helping women with unplanned pregnancies to have other options that are better than abortion. We can create new hope by providing the support necessary to make it possible for a woman to complete a pregnancy and perhaps even keep her baby. We can encourage her family to accept and support her if she is unmarried, rather than throw her out. We can urge the baby's father to take responsibility. Or we can work for social programs that will provide financial support and child care for single mothers. If the mother needs to complete her education to qualify for a suitable job, we can lobby for governmental assistance or church support to provide necessary programs and funding.

To establish laws against abortion might prove partially effective in reducing their numbers, but it would be the way of pride, not the way of servanthood and humility. The message would be, ''We are righteous. You who disobey our law are sinners.'' This kind of self-righteousness is pharisaical, a condemnation that excuses us from getting involved in actually helping a pregnant woman or her baby. Jesus' approach would be servanthood.

The well-known male activists with their dramatic campaigns to ''stop abortion'' are behaving like Jesus' disciples when they argued over who is greatest.[15] Jesus warned against those who

---

[15] Examples are Francis A. Schaeffer and C. Everett Koop, *Whatever Happened to the Human Race?* (Westchester, IL: Crossway Books, 1978); John W. Whitehead, *Arresting Abortion: Practical Ways to Save Unborn Children* (Westchester, IL: Crossway Books, 1985); Jerry Falwell, *If I Should Die*

sound trumpets in the synagogues and in the streets "that they may be praised by men." His judgment was, "Truly, I say to you, they have their reward" (Mt 6:2). They will gain the public acclaim they so obviously seek, but true reward from God will come to those who serve in humble, unseen ways. On the abortion issue, Jesus would probably say that the greatest in the eyes of God is the one who provides medical care, counseling, or financial support—helping just one woman regain physical and psychological strength if she chooses abortion—or helping her to find the necessary resources if she decides to keep the baby.

Persevere in Prayer

Besides speaking with gentleness and working in servanthood, the Bible counsels us to deal with a fallen world by persevering in prayer. If we want to reduce the number of abortions occurring annually, we must use the resource of prayer—for individuals, for clinics and their staff, and for all those faced with unwanted pregnancies.

A popular bumper sticker says, "Pray to stop abortion." I wish both sides would take this admonition seriously. Only prayer can really *stop* abortion for only God's Spirit can change lives, working deeply into our hearts and convicting us of concrete steps we can take to bring about God's peaceable kingdom. No Supreme Court decisions or legislation will ever stop abortion. They will only send it underground again, where organized crime syndicates will control and profit from it, and women's lives will be lost.

Before I Wake (New York: Nelson, 1986); Joseph M. Scheidler, *Closed: 99 Ways to Stop Abortion,* (Westchester, IL: Crossway Books, 1985).

Prayer plus servanthood are the truly Christian approach to reducing the abortion rate. In prayer God speaks to us and lays things on our hearts; we listen and grow. If Christians really undertook serious prayer on the problem of abortion, we could change our nation much more profoundly than by simply passing a federal law.

Conclusion

Our advocacy of procreative choice is grounded in biblical principles and theology. But theology and theory usually do not cause people to revise their positions on social issues. Concrete experiences—especially those that contradict or challenge long-held theories—push us to rethink our views and reexamine our theology. Since most of our legislators and many anti-abortion activists are male, they have not had the experience of facing an unplanned, unwanted pregnancy. Many women have also been blessed with a life in which all their children were wanted children or were "surprises" that could be added to a family without undue strain.

For these men and women, the personal stories in this book can provide a glimpse of the conflicts faced by sincere Christian women who have conceived a child they feel unable to bear and raise. Not everyone reading this book will conclude that abortion should remain legal, but at least all will gain food for thought and will grow in their sensitivity to women in crisis.

Organizations and
Resources §

Religious Coalition for Reproductive Choice (RCRC)
1025 Vermont Avenue NW, #1130
Washington, D.C. 20005   (202) 628-7700

Local organizations in most states
Publications:
- *RCRC Newsletter*
- *Words of Choice*
- *We Affirm: National Religious Organizations' Statements on Abortion Rights*
- "Abortion: Why religious organizations want to keep it legal"
- "Respecting the Moral Agency of Women" by Dr. Virginia Ramey Mollenkott
- "Is the fetus a person—according to the Bible?" by Dr. Roy Bowen Ward

Catholics for a Free Choice (CFFC)
1436 U Street NW, Suite 301
Washington, D.C. 20009-3997   202-986-6093

Local organizations in many states
Publications:
- *Conscience: A Newsjournal of Prochoice Catholic Opinion*
- *The History of Abortion in the Catholic Church*
- *The Church in a Democracy: Who Governs?*
- *Pro-Choice Catholics Testify: I Support You but I Can't Sign My Name*
- *Abortion: A Guide to Making Ethical Choices*

Planned Parenthood Federation of America, Inc. (PPFA)
810 Seventh Avenue
New York, NY 10019   (212) 541-7800

Local organizations in most counties
Publications:
- Newsletters in most counties
- Numerous flyers and booklets printed nationally and locally.

National Abortion Rights Action League (NARAL)
1101 - 14th Street NW
Washington, D.C. 20005   (202) 408-4600

Local organizations in most states
Publications:
- *NARAL Newsletter*
- Local newsletters in many states

National Organization for Women (NOW)
1000 16th Street
Washington, D.C. 20036-5705   (202) 331-0066

Local organizations in every state
Publications:
- *National NOW Times*
- Booklets and flyers.

Presbyterians Affirming Reproductive Options (PARO)
100 Witherspoon St.
Louisville, KY 40202-1396   (402) 569-5794

Common Ground Network for Life and Choice
1601 Connecticut Avenue NW, #200
Washington, DC 20009   (202) 265-4300

Evangelical and Ecumenical Women's Caucus
P.O. Box 9989
Oakland, CA 94613   (510) 635-5098

Local organizations in some states
Publications:
• *EEWC Newsletter*

Daughters of Sarah
2121 Sheridan Rd.
Evanston, IL 60201   (708) 866-3882

Publication:
• *Daughters of Sarah: The Magazine for Christian Feminists*

Note: The last three organizations maintain neutrality on the abortion issue in order to foster dialogue among feminists who have differing points of view.

Selected Books on
the Abortion Issue §

Bonavoglia, Angela, ed. *The Choices We Made: Twenty-Five Women and Men Speak Out about Abortion.* New York: Random House, 1991.

Cozic, Charles P. and Stacey L. Tipp, eds. *Abortion: Opposing Viewpoints.* San Diego: Greenhaven Press, 1991.

Feldman, David M. *Marital Relations, Birth Control, and Abortion in Jewish Law.* New York: Schocken Books, 1968.

Gorman, Michael J. *Abortion and the Early Church: Christian, Jewish and Pagan Attitudes in the Greco-Roman World.* New York: Paulist Press and InterVarsity Press, 1982.

Harrison, Beverly Wildung. *Our Right To Choose: Toward a New Ethic of Abortion.* Boston: Beacon Press, 1983.

Hoshiko, Sumi. *Our Choices: Women's Personal Decisions about Abortion.* Binghamton, NY: Harrington Park Press, 1993.

Luker, Kristin. *Abortion and the Politics of Motherhood.* Berkeley: Univ. of Calif. Press, 1984.

Petchesky, Rosalind Pollack. *Abortion and Woman's Choice: The State, Sexuality, and Reproductive Freedom.* Boston: Northeastern Univ. Press, 1984.

Anne Eggebroten has taught writing and literature at several colleges in the Los Angeles area. She earned her AB from Stanford University and her MA and Ph.D. from the University of California at Berkeley. A founding member of the Evangelical and Ecumenical Caucus in 1974, she is married and has three daughters, now twelve, nine, and seven. Her articles, book reviews and poems have appeared in *Christianity Today, Daughters of Sarah, The EEWC Update, The Other Side, Faith at Work, Christianity & Literature,* and two journals of medieval literature. In 1979 she contributed a chapter to *Our Struggle To Serve: The Stories of 15 Evangelical Women* edited by Virginia Hearn (Waco, Texas: Word, 1979). She has been a member of the National Organization for Women (NOW) since 1970.

Additional copies of this book may be obtained
from your local bookstore
or by sending $14.95 for a paperback copy, postpaid
or $21.95 for a library hardcover copy, postpaid
to:

New Paradigm Books
P.O. Box 60008
Pasadena, CA 91116

CA residents kindly add 8¼% tax
FAX orders to (818) 792-2121
VISA/MC orders to (800) 326-2671